The Basics

of Bible Prophecy

Darryl Nunnelley
and
David R. Reagan

www.lamblion.com

Dedicated to

Darryl Nunnelley's Mother and Father,
Carl & Clara Nunnelley

and his former minister and spiritual mentor,
Jim Bird

in appreciation for their encouragement,
teaching and Christian examples.

First edition, 2018

Copyright © 2018 by Lamb & Lion Ministries

ISBN: 978-0-945593-30-0

Library of Congress Control Number: 2018936717

Lamb & Lion Ministries
P.O. Box 919
McKinney, Texas 75070
lamblion@lamblion.com
www.lamblion.com

Cover design by Jana Olivieri.

All scripture quotations, unless otherwise noted, are from the New American Standard
Version, © 1995 by the Lockman Foundation.

Other Bible versions quoted:
TLB — *The Living Bible* (Tyndale House, 1971).
NIV — *The New International Version* (Zondervan, revised edition, 2011).
NKJV — *The New King James Version* (HarperCollins, 1982).
NLT — *The New Living Translation* (Tyndale House, revised edition, 2015).

Printed in the United States of America.

Contents

Books by Dr. David R. Reagan

The Christ in Prophecy Study Guide (McKinney, TX: Lamb & Lion Ministries, 1987). Second edition in 2001.

Trusting God: Learning to Walk by Faith (Lafayette, LA: Huntington House, 1987). Second edition in 1994 by Lamb & Lion Ministries. Third edition in 2015.

Jesus is Coming Again! (Eugene, OR: Harvest House, 1992). Second edition by Lamb & Lion Ministries in 2015.

The Master Plan: Making Sense of the Controversies Surrounding Bible Prophecy Today (Eugene, OR: Harvest House, 1993).

Living for Christ in the End Times (Green Forest, AR: New Leaf Press, 2000). Second edition in 2015 by Lamb & Lion Ministries.

Wrath and Glory: Unveiling the Majestic Book of Revelation (Green Forest, AR: New Leaf Press, 2001). Second edition in 2016 by Lamb & Lion.

America the Beautiful? The United States in Bible Prophecy (McKinney, TX: Lamb & Lion Ministries, 2003). Second edition in 2006. Third edition in 2009.

God's Plan for the Ages: The Blueprint of Bible Prophecy (McKinney, TX: Lamb & Lion Ministries, 2005).

Eternity: Heaven or Hell? (McKinney, TX: Lamb & Lion Ministries, 2010).

Jesus: The Lamb and The Lion (McKinney, TX: Lamb & Lion Ministries, 2011).

The Man of Lawlessness: The Antichrist in the Tribulation (McKinney, TX: Lamb & Lion Ministries, 2012).

A Prophetic Manifesto (McKinney, TX: Lamb & Lion Ministries, 2012).

Living on Borrowed Time: The Imminent Return of Jesus (McKinney, TX: Lamb & Lion Ministries, 2013).

The Jewish People: Rejected or Beloved? (McKinney, TX: Lamb & Lion Ministries, 2014).

Israel in Bible Prophecy: Past, Present & Future (McKinney, TX: Lamb & Lion Ministries, 2017).

God's Prophetic Voices to America (McKinney, TX: Lamb & Lion Ministries, 2017).

Preface

One of the trustees of Lamb & Lion Ministries, Darryl Nunnelley of Winchester, Kentucky, was the one who came to me with the idea for this book.

Darryl had been involved for many years in teaching an overview of the Bible, using a teaching book by Orin Root titled, *A Survey of the Bible: Training for Service* (Cincinnati, OH: Standard Publishing, revised edition in 1998). Darryl suggested that we work together to produce a similar book that would focus on teaching the fundamentals of Bible prophecy. I liked the idea, and I accepted the challenge.

I asked Darryl to formulate a statement of purpose, and he did so as follows:

> This generation is blessed with so many books and other study aids of the Bible, from overviews to extremely in-depth analyses in many formats. Students of the Bible from the beginner to the accomplished scholar can easily find many resources for their particular needs.

> But this does not seem to be the case for Bible prophecy, which amounts to almost 30 percent of the Bible. Yes, there are many resources that reach even into the deepest principles of prophetic views and beliefs. Yet, I have not found a brief overview study guide for Sunday Schools, small groups, Christian and Home Schools, and individuals that can lead a new prophecy student through the process of beginning to understand God's Prophetic Word.

> God gave us prophecy for the same reason He gave us all the other parts of His Word. He wants us to know the future, as well as the past, and how it affects us. It is my prayer that this book will:

> - Provide a basis for understanding God's Prophetic Word.

> - Make the study of Bible prophecy easier, enlightening and enjoyable.

> - Demonstrate how Bible prophecy is relevant to Christian living here and now.

> - Emphasize that we are living in the season of the Lord's return.

> - Provide both the information and format that will enable the book to be used to teach the fundamentals of Bible prophecy.

Darryl contributed much more than just the idea for this book. He also provided the outline of the lessons, and he wrote the first drafts for each chapter. I then took his drafts and used them to produce the final text. It was a true team effort.

Our approach from start to finish has been based on the belief that Bible prophecy means what it says. We have therefore interpreted it for its literal or plain sense meaning, unless it is clearly symbolic, in which case we have sought to provide the clear meaning of the symbol. Many, if not most, churches today teach that the prophecies of the end times related to the Second Coming of Jesus do not mean what they say. But all the First Coming prophecies meant what they said, and therefore we believe that the Second Coming prophecies also mean what they say, as we clearly teach in Lesson 4.

Bible prophecy has been terribly abused by some and ignored by most, and that is a real shame because the study of it will motivate holiness and evangelism. It also builds hope, something that is desperately needed in the dark world in which we live today. In that regard, the great pastor and preacher, Adrian Rogers (1931-2005) once said: "The world is growing gloriously dark." There is no way that anyone can understand this very insightful statement without a knowledge of Bible prophecy.

The hope Darryl and I share with regard to this book is that it will be a blessing to each person who reads it and that what it contains will draw them into a deeper relationship with the Lord Jesus Christ.

Maranatha!

Dave Reagan
McKinney, Texas
Spring of 2018

> *Blessed is the one who reads aloud the words of this prophecy, and blessed are those who hear it and take to heart what is written in it, because the time is near* (Revelation 1:3 – NIV).

Lesson 1

The Importance of Bible Prophecy

> **Fact:** *Bible prophecy is an essential part of God's Word.*

Key Scripture: *"So we have seen and proved that what the prophets said came true. You will do well to pay close attention to everything they have written, for, like lights shining into dark corners, their words help us to understand many things that otherwise would be dark and difficult . . ."* (2 Peter 1:19 – TLB)

Definitions of Bible Prophecy:

- Holy Spirit inspired utterances regarding the future (2 Peter 1:20-21).

- History written in advance (Daniel 2:31-45).

- God-breathed foretelling of His will (2 Timothy 3:16).

- The application of God's Word to the sins of society (Amos 5:21-24).

Reasons to Study Prophecy

1) We worship a God of Prophecy.

Isaiah 46:9-11

9) ". . . I am God, and there is no other; I am God, and there is no one like Me,

10) Declaring the end from the beginning, and from ancient times things which have not been done, saying, 'My purpose will be established, and I will accomplish all My good pleasure;'

11) . . . Truly I have spoken; truly I will bring it to pass. I have planned it, surely I will do it."

God is saying that He is the one and only true God and that He can prove it because He has the wisdom to know the future, the audacity to proclaim it, and the power to see to it that what He declares comes to pass.

2) Fulfilled prophecy assures us of God's sovereignty.

Psalm 103:19

The LORD has established His throne in the heavens, And His sovereignty rules over all.

When we see Bible prophecy fulfilled, we can be assured that God is on His throne and is in full control of history. We can be confident that He has the wisdom and power to orchestrate all the evil of Mankind and Satan to the triumph of His Son in history (Psalm 2:1-6).

3) Fulfilled prophecy validates the Bible as the Word of God.

The Bible is the only book in the world that contains fulfilled prophecies. There are none in the Quran, the Hindu Vedas or the Book of Mormon. There are hundreds of Bible prophecies concerning persons, cities, nations and empires which have already been fulfilled.

Fulfilled prophecies attest to the supernatural origin of the Bible. Unbelievers and Christian liberals argue that the Bible is Man's search for God. Fulfilled prophecies prove the Bible is God's revelation to Man (Isaiah 37:26).

4) The quantity of prophecy in the Bible demands its attention.

Between one-fourth and one-third of the Bible is prophetic in nature. According to J. Barton Payne's *Encyclopedia of Biblical Prophecy*, there are 6,641 verses in the Old Testament and 1,711 in the New Testament that contain predictive material. Are all these verses simply to be put on the shelve and ignored?

In 1 Thessalonians 5:20, the Apostle Paul wrote: "Do not despise prophecies" (NKJV).

5) Prophecy validates Jesus as God in the flesh.

An angel from Heaven declared to the Apostle John that prophecy is a witness of Jesus' divinity: "For the testimony of Jesus is the spirit of prophecy" (Revelation 19:10).

Jesus fulfilled 109 separate and distinct prophecies in His First Coming. The odds of any person doing that accidentally is beyond the realm of probability.

6) Prophecy can be an effective tool of evangelism.

The very first Gospel sermon ever preached — the one by the Apostle Peter on the Day of Pentecost — was based on Bible prophecy from beginning to end (Acts 2:14-36).

Philip the Evangelist converted the Ethiopian Eunuch using Bible prophecy (Acts 8:26-39).

Literally thousands of people have proclaimed that they came to a belief in Jesus as their Lord and Savior through reading Hal Lindsey's book, *The Late Great Planet Earth*, which was published in 1970 and which remained the best selling book for ten consecutive years.

7) Prophecy can be an effective tool of moral teaching.

The biblical prophets did not spend all their time talking about the future. They spent much more time forth-telling the present than foretelling the future. This means they took the Word of God and applied it to the contemporary problems of their day, like denouncing idolatry and hypocrisy.

- Idolatry: Isaiah 44:9-20 and Jeremiah 10:1-16.

- Hypocrisy: Jeremiah 7:8-11 and Amos 5:21-24.

8) Prophecy can be a stimulus for spiritual growth.

When people start truly believing two prophetic truths, their lives will be drastically changed. Those two truths are that Jesus is returning to this earth and that His return is an event that could occur any moment. Those who believe these two prophetic truths will commit their lives to holiness and evangelism.

Consider these four prophetic passages that link one's attitude about the Lord's return to spiritual preparation:

- Romans 13:11-14
- 1 Timothy 6:11-14
- Titus 2:11-14
- 1 Peter 4:7-13

9) Prophecy provides insights concerning current world events.

Those who know Bible prophecy

are not bewildered by the increase in immorality and violence, the never-ending crisis in the Middle East, and the raging apostasy in the Church. All these things are clearly prophesied for the end times. Consider:

- The disintegration of society: Matthew 24:37-38 and 2 Timothy 3:1-5.

- The crisis in the Middle East: Zechariah 12:1-3, 6-9.

- The increasing apostasy in the Church: 2 Timothy 4:1-4 and 2 Peter 2:1-3.

10) Prophecy provides hope.

Romans 8:18

"For I consider that the sufferings of this present time are not worthy to be compared with the glory that is to be revealed to us."

Bible prophecy is full of glorious future promises for believers. Examples:

- Resurrection of the dead: 1 Corinthians 15:42-44, 51-55.

- Rewards for works: Matthew 16:27 and Revelation 22:12.

- New glorified bodies: Isaiah 35:5-6 and Philippians 3:20-21.

- Reigning over the world with Jesus: 2 Timothy 2:11-12 and Revelation 5:9-10.

- Victory over Satan: Revelation 20:7-10.

- Eternal life: Matthew 25:31-46 and John 17:1-3.

The Return of Jesus

Certainly, one of the most important reasons for studying Bible prophecy is because it contains signs we are to watch for which will indicate the season of the Lord's return. We cannot know the date (Matthew 24:36 and 1 Thessalonians 5:1-3), but we can know the season (1 Thessalonians 5:4-6, Hebrews 10:25 and Matthew 24:33). ✤

Quotations:

"I've read the last page of the Bible. It's all going to turn out all right." — Billy Graham (1918-2018).

"Bible prophecy helps us to better understand the future and realize the urgent need to spread the Gospel. It motivates us to personal purity and gives us hope in a hopeless age." — Tim LaHaye (1926-2016).

". . . if you are aware of Christ's imminent return, that will impact your desire to witness to others about the Gospel. If we take prophecy seriously, it will affect the way we live. Some of the most energetic people I know in the Church have been transformed by their study of prophecy. They're ministry oriented, reaching out to the lost because they understand what will happen in the future. Prophecy is intensely practical — it is the driving force behind evangelism and righteous living." — David Jeremiah, pastor of Shadow Mountain Community Church in El Cajon, California.

Questions:

1) Why do you think God devoted so much of His Word to prophecy?

_____

_____

2) What are some of the fulfilled prophecies that help you to have complete trust in the Bible?

_____

_____

3) Read Revelation 19:10. Why do you think God made Jesus the focus of prophecy?

_____

_____

4) How might you use prophecy for sharing the Gospel?

_____

_____

5) Read Titus 2:11-14. Some have called these verses a "spiritual mirror." List below the things they say we are to be doing as we wait for the Lord's return. Are you doing these things?

_____

_____

6) Many Christians have written off Bible prophecy as a legitimate focus of study because they say, "Bible prophecy is a playground for fanatics." Do you consider this a good reason for avoiding a study of Bible prophecy?

_____

_____

_____

7) In the very first Gospel sermon ever preached, the Apostle Peter quoted five Old Testament prophecies. Read Acts 2:14-36 and identify the sources of the five prophecies he quoted.

_____

_____

_____

Lesson 2

The Abuse of Bible Prophecy

> **Fact:** *Bible prophecy has been one of the most ignored and abused portions of God's Word.*

Key Scripture: *". . . you should remember the words spoken before hand by the holy prophets and the commandments of the Lord and Savior spoken by your apostles. Know this first of all, that in the last days mockers will come with their mocking, following after their own lusts, and saying, 'Where is the promise of His coming?'"* (2 Peter 3:3-4)

Reasons Given
for Ignoring Prophecy

"It's too complex. You have to have a degree in theology to understand it."

Yes, it takes study. But God desires to communicate His will and one does not need theological training to understand God's Word, anymore than the Apostles, many of whom were uneducated fishermen. What you do need is the indwelling of the Holy Spirit (John 14:26) and a willingness to study (2 Timothy 2:15).

"It's too other-worldly."

Then why did the Apostles use it constantly in their teaching and preaching? (Acts 2:14-36 and 1 Thessalonians 4:13-18)

"It's all pie-in-the-sky."

No, it's full of God's precious promises concerning the future (1 Corinthians 2:7-10).

"It's divisive."

It can be, if it is taught dogmatically, with arrogance — just as is the case with any other portion of God's Word (Colossians 3:12-17 and Titus 2:7-8).

"It's Old Testament."

Jesus revered and quoted the Old Testament prophecies (Matthew 4:1-11 and Matthew 24:15-21), and we are exhorted to pay attention to the teachings of the Old Testament (1 Corinthians 10:1-12).

Also, keep in mind that the New Testament is full of passages that quote and reaffirm Old Testament prophecies (Matthew 1:19-23 and Acts 15:14-19).

"It doesn't apply to me."

Who says? John the Baptist presented a prophecy in John 3:36 that applies to every person who has ever lived — namely, that those who put their faith in Jesus will have eternal life, and those who do not will experience the wrath of God.

Prophecy is full of warnings to unbelievers and "precious promises" for those who have put their faith in Jesus (Hebrews 3:12 and 2 Peter 1:4).

"It's all too scary. It's full of bad news."

Yes, there are a lot of terrible and frightening prophecies, but only for those who reject God's gift of love and grace in Jesus. For those who accept Jesus as their Lord and Savior, there is only good news — gloriously good news (Revelation 20:6).

"If it's for real, then why hasn't Jesus returned?"

Good question. And the answer is given by the Apostle Peter in 2 Peter 3:3-9 where he explains that the only reason Jesus has not returned is because God "does not wish that any should perish, but that all should come to repentance."

"If it's for real, then why are there so many prophecies that have not been fulfilled?"

The only prophecies that have not been fulfilled are those that relate to the future — to the Tribulation, the Second Coming, the Millennium and the Eternal State. Just as hundreds of other prophecies have been fulfilled that relate to the past, these will also be fulfilled when the time comes.

Ways in Which Prophecy Has Been Abused

1) The Apostates

These are people who profess to be Christians but who deny that the Bible contains any prophecy. They dismiss prophetic passages either as meaningless poetry or else they argue that the prophecies were written after the event that was prophesied. The bottom line is that they reject the supernatural inspiration of the Bible. The very existence of such people in the Church today is a fulfillment of Bible prophecies (Matthew 24:10-12, 2 Timothy 3:1,5 and 2 Peter 3:1-4).

2) The Spiritualizers

These are Christians who argue that prophecy never means what it says. So, they spiritualize it to mean whatever they want it to mean — in which case, they play God. If prophecy does not mean what it says, then how can we ever know when it is fulfilled? Prophecy, like all of God's Word, must be interpreted for its plain sense meaning. And yes, prophecy often contains symbols, but they have a literal meaning, and that meaning is often revealed in the passage itself, as in Revelation 1:13,16, 20.

3) The Fanatics

These are Christians who really believe in Bible prophecy but who seem obsessed in using it to engage in wild speculations about the future, including such things as the identity of the Antichrist and the date of the Lord's return. Their irresponsible manipulation of prophecies is what has caused many people to hold prophecy in contempt.

4) The Apathetic

These are Christians who simply couldn't care less. They are either cold in the faith, or they are too lazy to study God's Prophetic Word. They often just shrug their shoulders and say, "I'm a Pan-millennialist because I believe it will all just pan out in the end." Sad!

Prophecy is an Expression of God's Love

Prophecy was given to warn us about future events and to prepare us for them, not to scare us. Informing us about the future through prophecy is an expression of God's love for us.

His desire is for us to be able to understand end time events, to endure and to have the hope of total victory when Jesus returns. Also, we are to share His prophetic truths and their fulfillments to convince people that the only hope for this world is Jesus, the Messiah.

In 1 Corinthians 2:9-10a, we find these words:

> As it is written,
> "No eye has seen,
> no ear has heard,
> no mind has conceived
> what God has prepared
> for those who love Him"
> — but God has revealed it to
> us by His Spirit (NIV).

Paul is quoting Isaiah 64:4 in an effort to point out that the blessings God has prepared for believers are so great that they are beyond our imagination, yet many have been revealed by the Holy Spirit through prophecies.

A Satanic Conspiracy

Satan does not want anyone studying prophecy, because prophecy contains the revelation of Satan's ultimate and total defeat, while revealing the absolute victory of Jesus.

The wonderful message of Bible prophecy for believers is that *"We win in the end!"* Satan does not want anyone to know that message. And thus, Satan has inspired the abuse of God's Prophetic Word. The less we know of God's Prophetic Word, the more deception Satan can employ.

The Apostles Paul and Peter commanded us to respect and pay attention to prophecy (1 Thessalonians 5:20 and 2 Peter 1:19). ✤

Quotation:

"A very striking and strange condition exists at present, namely, the deliberate refusal on the part of religious leaders to consult carefully the prophetic Scriptures. True, there have been cranks, blind fanatics, hobby-riders and unwise date-setters posing as prophetic teachers, but all of these unscholarly obscurantists put together do not afford any man a legitimate excuse for not studying the divine plan as it is plainly set forth in the Bible." — Lehman Strauss (1911-1997), pastor and author.

Questions:

1) Have you been ignoring Bible prophecy? If so, why?

_____

2) Why do you think so many pastors ignore the teaching of Bible prophecy?

_____

_____

3) What do you think is the most important reason to study Bible prophecy?

_____

_____

4) What is your favorite Bible prophecy scripture, and why?

_____

Lesson 3

The Varieties of Prophecy

> **Fact:** *God used a great variety of people, methods and literary styles to communicate His Prophetic Word.*

Key Scripture: *"God, after He spoke long ago to the fathers in the prophets in many portions and in many ways, in these last days has spoken to us in His Son, whom He appointed heir of all things, through whom also He made the world"* (Hebrews 1:1-2).

God Loves Variety

God created over 10,000 species of birds, over 31,500 species of fish, over 287,600 species of plants and more than 1,250,000 species of animals. He also created many different races, nations, languages, cultures, land forms, chemical elements, etc. His love of variety is reflected in both the types of people and the forms of communication He used to express His Prophetic Word.

The Prophets

They ranged from an uneducated farmer, Amos, to sophisticated poets like Isaiah; from reluctant spokesmen like Jonah to men of great courage like Daniel; and from little known Joel to famous personalities like King David. Some, like Zechariah, were very young, while others, like Haggai, were elderly.

The Sources

Most of the prophets relied on direct revelations — "Thus says the Lord." Others received their insights through dreams and visions. Some, like Hosea and Jonah, simply recorded their experiences.

The Styles

The writing prophets resorted to a great variety of written forms. Some, like Ezekiel, Daniel, Haggai and the New Testament prophets, primarily used a prose style. Others, like David, Isaiah, Joel and Micah, expressed their ideas in poetic form. And then there are the preachers whose books are mainly collections of sermons — prophets like Jeremiah, Amos, and Zechariah.

Other Forms of Expression

In addition to the writing prophets, there were oral prophets who wrote nothing at all. We know about them because others wrote about their revelations, pronouncements and exploits. Elijah and his successor, Elisha, fall into this category.

Sometimes, God would speak to an oral prophet or a writing prophet and tell them to stop speaking and writing and to concentrate instead on communicating through acting.

And then there is what is called "symbolic prophecy" or "prophecy in type." This occurs when a person's life or a historical event or even an inanimate object is symbolic of something that is going to happen in the future.

Oral Prophets

Generally speaking the oral prophets are less well known than those who wrote the prophetic books of the Bible. And yet, the greatest prophet who ever lived was an oral prophet — Jesus of Nazareth. The only writings of Jesus that exist are His seven letters to the seven churches of Asia, recorded by John in Revelation 2 and 3. The bulk of Jesus' prophecies, like His Olivet Discourse (Matthew 24, Mark 13, and Luke 21), were recorded in written form by His disciples.

Only a few oral prophets are mentioned in the New Testament — like the four daughters of Philip (Acts 21:8-9) and Agabus, the prophet who counseled Paul (Acts 21:10-11).

But the Old Testament is full of oral prophets. There is Nathan, who confronted David (2 Samuel 12); Micaiah, who saw the Lord sitting on His throne (1 Kings 22); Ahijah, who condemned Jeroboam (1 Kings 14); Hananiah, the false prophet who spoke against Jeremiah (Jeremiah 28); and many nameless prophets like the "man of God from Judah" who prophesied the birth of Josiah (1 Kings 13).

Acting Prophets

God often used drama to get people's attention. For example, He told Isaiah to go barefoot and naked for three years (Isaiah 20:2-3). Yes, Isaiah was the original streaker! The message was graphic and clear: Repent or be stripped naked like Isaiah.

Jeremiah was told to wear an oxen yoke on his neck to emphasize God's message that King Zedekiah should submit to Nebuchadnezzar (Jeremiah 27).

Ezekiel was called on to act many times. On one occasion the Lord told him to pack all his bags and carry them around Jerusalem in the sight of the people as a sign that if they did not repent, God would send them into exile (Ezekiel 12:1-6).

On another occasion God ordered Ezekiel to play in a sand pile! God told him to label a brick, "Jerusalem," and to build dirt ramps around the brick to illustrate the coming siege of the city, if the people did not repent (Ezekiel 4:1-3).

The greatest actor of all, the one who will undoubtedly win the prophetic Oscar for best performance, was the prophet Hosea.

God told this righteous preacher to find a prostitute and marry her. Hosea did what God said. Later she abandoned him and went back to her sinful ways. God told Hosea to find her and pay whatever it took to redeem her from prostitution.

The message was that Israel was like that prostitute when God selected the nation as His Chosen People. They were not selected for their beauty or wisdom or righteousness. They had no merit of their own. They were selected by grace. Further, the message was that — like Hosea's wife — Israel had been unfaithful to God, chasing after foreign gods. And like Hosea, God's heart was broken.

Yet, like Hosea, God was willing to forgive and forget and pay the price of redemption in Israel's behalf, just as He is willing to do for us today. And thus the story of Hosea is the story of the Gospel.

Symbolic Prophecy

An understanding of prophetic types is essential to understanding the Old Testament. Jesus can be found on almost every page of the Old Testament, if you know how to look for Him. He is there symbolically in types. Looking for Him and finding Him in these types causes the Old Testament to come alive. This is most likely the kind of special teaching that Jesus gave His disciples during the 40 days between His resurrection and His ascension (Luke 24:45).

There are three kinds of prophetic types: 1) individual lives, 2) historical events and 3) inanimate objects.

1) Symbolic Persons

Almost all the major persons in the Old Testament are types of Christ in the sense that some events in their lives prophesied things that would happen to Jesus.

Take Joseph for example. He was rejected by his brothers. He was left for dead but was "resurrected" from the pit into which he had been cast. He took a Gentile bride and then redeemed his brothers from their famine.

Likewise, Jesus was rejected by his brethren (the Jews), experienced death and resurrection, is now taking a Gentile Bride (the Church), and will soon return to save a remnant of His brethren from their spiritual famine.

2) Symbolic Events

The history of the Jewish nation is the story of Jesus in prophetic type. The Children of Israel were born in Canaan, migrated to Egypt, came through the Red Sea (the baptism of Moses), endured testing in the wilderness, and then entered the Promised Land.

Likewise, Jesus was born in Canaan, was taken to Egypt, emerged publicly at His baptism, endured the wilderness temptations, and led the way to Heaven.

3) Symbolic Objects

Even inanimate objects like the Tabernacle of Moses and the robe of the High Priest are prophetic types pointing to Jesus.

Consider the Ark of the Covenant. Everything about it was symbolic of the Messiah. It was made of wood, indicating the Messiah would be human. It was overlaid with gold, signifying the Messiah would be divine. It contained three objects — the tablets of stone, a pot of manna, and Aaron's rod that budded. The tablets signified that the Messiah would have the law of God in His heart. The manna meant the Messiah would be the Bread of Life. The rod with blooms was a prophecy that the Messiah would arise from the dead.

The lid of the Ark was called the Mercy Seat. It had a golden angel at each end. The angels faced each other and their wings hovered over the lid. Once a year the High Priest sprinkled blood on the Mercy Seat and communed with the Shekinah glory of God which hovered above the angels.

The Mercy Seat pointed to the fact that through the work of the Messiah the mercy of God would cover the Law. The blood foreshadowed the fact that the Messiah would have to shed His own blood to atone for our sins.

Jesus fulfilled every prophetic type of the Ark. He was God in the flesh (John 10:30). He had the Law in His heart (Matthew 5:17). He declared Himself to be the "Bread of Life" (John 6:35). He shed His blood on the Cross and was resurrected in power, atoning for our sins and covering the Law with Grace (Romans 3:21-26).

An Exhortation

Read the Bible with an attitude of always looking for Jesus. He is there on almost every page, waiting for you to discover Him in the symbols and types.

Pray for the guidance of the Holy Spirit as you read, and remember Revelation 19:10 — "The testimony of Jesus is the spirit of prophecy." ✠

Questions:

1) Study the chart of the Jewish Feasts on page 18. Notice how each feast is prophetic in nature, either about the life of Jesus or the future of the Church.

    a) Which ones have already been fulfilled? _____

    b) Which ones are yet to be fulfilled? _____

2) Read the brief book of Jonah.

    a) How is it prophetic in reference to the life of Jesus?

    _____

    b) Confirm your answer with a quote from Jesus in the New Testament:

    _____

3) Read Ezekiel 22:1-12 and 25-31. These verses contain an indictment of the people of Judah and Jerusalem. What sins listed there can be found in our nation today?

_____

_____

_____

4) Read Ezekiel 24:15-24 where God asks Ezekiel to do a very strange and unnatural thing. What is the message that he acts out?

_____

_____

5) Read 1 Kings 22:1-28. Note what oral prophets are mentioned in these verses and how their messages differed. _____

_____

_____

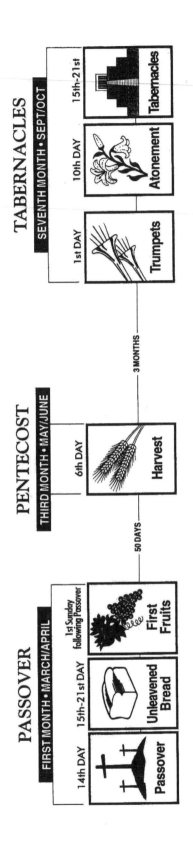

PASSOVER
FIRST MONTH • MARCH/APRIL

14th DAY	15th-21st DAY	1st Sunday following Passover
Passover	Unleavened Bread	First Fruits

— 50 DAYS —

PENTECOST
THIRD MONTH • MAY/JUNE

6th DAY
Harvest

— 3 MONTHS —

TABERNACLES
SEVENTH MONTH • SEPT/OCT

1st DAY	10th DAY	15th-21st
Trumpets	Atonement	Tabernacles

FEAST — CHRISTIAN EVENT — KEY CONCEPT

FEAST	CHRISTIAN EVENT	KEY CONCEPT
Passover	Crucifixion of Jesus	Justification
Unleavened Bread	Burial of Jesus	Sanctification
First Fruits	Resurrection of Jesus	Glorification
Harvest	Descent of Holy Spirit	Power
Interval of 3 Months	Current Age of the Church	Church Kingdom
Trumpets	Gathering of the Church (?)	Rapture
Day of Atonement	Second Coming of Jesus (?)	Jewish Remnant
Tabernacles	Inauguration of the Millennium	Earthly Kingdom

Lesson 4

The Interpretation of Prophecy

> **Fact:** *Bible prophecy was meant to be understood by the common person.*

Key Scripture: *"Now we have received, not the spirit of the world, but the Spirit who is from God, so that we may know the things freely given to us by God, which things we also speak, not in words taught by human wisdom, but in those taught by the Spirit, combining spiritual thoughts with spiritual words"* (1 Corinthians 2:12-13).

Two Myths

Many people believe that Bible prophecy is indecipherable to anyone except theologians who have been trained at a seminary.

Others believe that Bible prophecy never means what it says, and they therefore spiritualize it to mean what they want it to say.

The Truth

God wants to communicate with us, and He knows how to do it. You do not have to be a seminary graduate to understand Bible prophecy.

Theologians refer to the principles of biblical interpretation as "hermeneutics," which causes most people to respond, "Herman who?" The word is derived from the Greek god, Hermes, who was considered to be the messenger of the gods.

It is important to realize that there is a God-given meaning to all Scripture, apart from any of our wishes or preconceived notions, and that meaning is determined by God. Understanding that meaning is the task of hermeneutics. What does it matter to believe that the Bible is God's perfect word if you misinterpret it? To draw God's intended meaning from the Scriptures, apart from anything else, is our task. Some principles for doing just that are listed below.

Principles of Interpretation

1) Have the Right Attitude:

The Scriptures need to be approached with childlike faith, believing that God wants us to understand what He is saying, and that when He speaks, He means what He says. Dr. Henry Morris addresses this issue in his great commentary on Revelation, called *The Revelation Record*. He says: "Revelation is not difficult to understand. It is difficult to believe. If you will believe it, you will understand it."

For example, in Revelation 7 it says that at the start of the Tribulation God is going to seal a great host of Jews to serve as His special "bond-servants." The text specifies that the number will be 144,000, and that 12,000 will be selected from each of 12 specified Jewish tribes.

What would God have to do to convince us that He intends to set aside 144,000 Jews for special service during the Tribulation? The text is crystal clear. Yet, hundreds of commentators have denied the clear meaning and have spiritualized the passage to make it refer to the Church! This is reckless handling of God's Word, and it produces nothing but confusion.

2) Look for the Surface Meaning:

Always look for the plain sense meaning of every passage. A good rule for the interpretation of all of Scripture, including prophecy, is this one: "If the plain sense makes sense, don't look for any other sense, lest you end up with nonsense."

Early in Christian history, due to the influence of Greek philosophy, some of the Church Fathers began to allegorize the Scriptures, arguing that the real meaning was hidden below the surface. This resulted in all kinds of fanciful interpretations.

The Bible is not written in code. The surface meaning is the true meaning. The First Coming prophecies about the Messiah meant what they said. There is no reason, therefore, to spiritualized the Second Coming prophecies. Thus, when Revelation 20 says that Jesus is going to return to this earth to reign for a thousand years, we should accept this to mean what it says.

3) Consider the Context:

Always keep in mind the context because context determines the meaning of words. A word in one context may be symbolic whereas in another context it may be literal.

For example, in Psalm 50:10 God says that "the cattle on a thousand hills" belong to Him. The context makes it clear that the word, thousand, is symbolic. But in Revelation 20 where we are told six times that

the Lord is returning to reign for a thousand years, the context makes it clear that the word, thousand, is literal.

4) Let Scripture Interpret Scripture:

Scripture is its own best interpreter. A correct interpretation is always consistent with all the rest of the Scriptures.

Revelation 13 says that in the middle of the Tribulation the Antichrist will attempt to annihilate the Jewish people, and many of them will escape on "the wings of a great eagle." Some have interpreted this to mean that the United States, whose symbol is an eagle, will supply an airlift to rescue the Jews. But this exact same terminology is used to describe the escape of the children of Israel from Egyptian captivity (Exodus 19:4 and Deuteronomy 32:11). All it means is that they escaped under the protection of God.

5) Reconcile all Scriptures:

Avoid hanging a doctrine on one isolated verse. All verses on a particular topic must be searched out, compared, and then reconciled.

Second Peter 3:10 says that when the Lord returns, "the heavens will pass away with a roar . . . and the earth and its works will be burned up." Now, if this were the only verse in the Bible about the Second Coming, we could confidently conclude that the heavens and earth will be burned up on the day that Jesus returns.

But, there are many other verses in both the Old and New Testaments, which make it abundantly clear that the Lord will reign over all the earth before it is consumed with fire. Those verses must be considered together with the passage in 2 Peter 3 in order to get the correct overall view.

6) Watch for Prophetic Gaps:

The previous example points to the fact that there are often gaps in Bible prophecy. This is due to what is called "telescoping." This occurs when a prophet compresses the time interval between prophetic events.

The reason this happens is due to the perspective of the prophet. As he looks into the future, he sees a series of events, but he does not necessarily see the time gaps between those events. It's like he is looking at a series of mountain tops and is unable to see the valleys between each peak. (See the illustration on page 22.)

In Zechariah 9:9-10 there is a passage with three prophecies which are compressed into two verses, but which are widely separated in time. Verse 9 says the Messiah will come humbly on a donkey. The first part of verse 10 says the Jewish people will be set aside. The second part of verse 10 says the Messiah will reign over all the nations.

These three events — the First Coming, the setting aside of Israel, and the reign of Christ — appear to occur in quick succession, but in reality, there were 40 years between the first two events, and there have been almost 2,000 years thus far between the second and third events.

7) Be Aware of Prefilling:

Sometimes prophecy is prefilled in symbolic type before it is completely fulfilled.

In this regard, the Jewish people must have felt that Antiochus Epiphanes (215 - 164 BC) fulfilled Daniel's prophecies about a tyrannical leader who would severely persecute the Jews. But 200 years after Antiochus, Jesus referred to those prophecies of Daniel and told His disciples they were yet to be fulfilled. Antiochus was a symbolic type of the Antichrist, but he was not the Antichrist.

8) Avoid "Unique" Interpretations:

Don't try to be the only one to ever "discover" a different interpretation of Scripture. If you do, you will most likely end up with a heresy.

Keep in mind the warning of 2 Peter 1:20-21, which says: "But know this first of all, that no prophecy of Scripture is a matter of one's own interpretation, for no prophecy was ever made by an act of human will, but men moved by the Holy Spirit spoke from God."

A Challenge

Mastering Bible prophecy requires time devoted to serious study. And it requires the study of all of God's Word — both the Old and New Testaments. But it will be time well spent because you will discover three things: 1) Fulfilled prophecy confirms that the Bible is the Word of God; 2) Fulfilled Messianic prophecy is proof positive that Jesus was the Son of God; and 3) Prophecies yet to be fulfilled provide hope for the future. ✤

Quotation: "About the time of the end, a body of men will be raised up who will turn their attention to the prophecies, and insist upon their literal interpretation in the midst of much clamor and opposition." — Sir Isaac Newton (1643-1727).

Questions:

1) When Jesus read Isaiah 61:1-2 in the synagogue in Nazareth (Luke 4:16-24), He stopped reading in the middle of verse 2. Why?

_____

_____

2) Read Zechariah 14:1-9. Does this passage mean what it says? If not, why not?

_____

_____

3) Read Isaiah 2:1-4. What do you think is the meaning of these verses?

_____

_____

_____

4) The First Coming prophecy in Micah 5:2 was fulfilled literally in the life of Jesus. Why would that not be true of the prophecy about the Lord's millennial reign contained in Micah 4:1-4?

_____

_____

Mountain Peaks of Bible Prophecy

The prophet sees events prophesied for the future but not the time intervals in between the events. Thus, they appear to him to be events that will occur immediately after each other.

Lesson 5

End Time Viewpoints

Fact: *There are four major ways in which end time Bible prophecy has been interpreted.*

Key Scripture: *"And I saw thrones, and they sat upon them, and judgment was given to them . . .* [and they] *reigned with Christ for a thousand years"* (Revelation 20:4).

The verse above is one of the most controversial in the Bible. Four major interpretations have been given to it.

Why the Differences?

It all has to do with the method of interpretation that is applied to the verse. If you interpret the verse for its plain sense meaning, you will end up with one of the forms of what is called Premillennialism. But if you desire to interpret the verse symbolically by spiritualizing its meaning, you will end up with one of the two views based upon such an approach.

Lets' consider the four views in the chronological order that they developed in history.

Historic Premillennialism

Don't let the word, premillennial, scare you. It just means "before the thousand years." It is the belief that Jesus will return to this earth before the Millennium begins. The Millennium is the thousand years referred to in the opening verse above.

This was the viewpoint of the early church up until the year 400

A.D. There is no disagreement about this. Even those who hold a different viewpoint agree that the view of the Church Fathers was that Jesus would return to this earth to reign for a thousand years. The view is diagramed on the next page — see figure 1.

So, according to this view, the Church Age that we are in now will be followed by a period of seven years called The Tribulation — a time when God will pour out His wrath upon the earth. Jesus will appear in the heavens at the end of the Tribulation. The saints, living and dead, will meet Him in the sky and return with Him to earth immediately to reign with Him from Jerusalem. At the end of His reign, this current earth will be renovated by fire, producing a new and perfected earth. The saints will then live with God eternally on the new earth.

This view is based upon a literal or plain sense interpretation of what the Bible says about the reign of Jesus on this earth.

Amillennialism

The second view was developed by Saint Augustine around 400 A.D. He is considered the greatest of the Church Fathers because his theology had the greatest impact on the doctrines that ultimately were adopted by

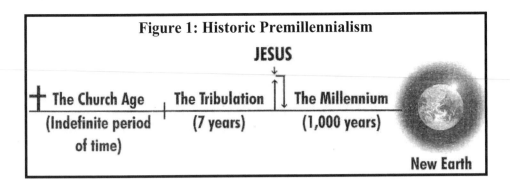

Figure 1: Historic Premillennialism

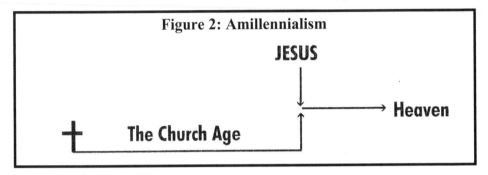

Figure 2: Amillennialism

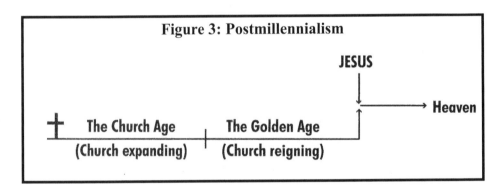

Figure 3: Postmillennialism

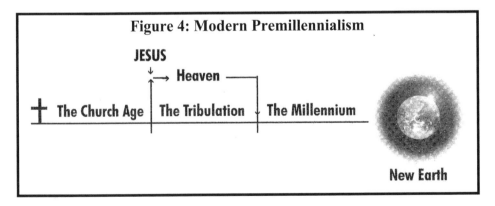

Figure 4: Modern Premillennialism

The Roman Catholic Church.

The concept formulated by Augustine is illustrated in Figure 2 on page 24. It is called Amillennialism. This strange name derives from the fact that in the Greek language a word is negated by putting the letter "a" in front of it. Thus, Amillennial literally means "no thousand years."

The term is misleading, however, because Amillennialists do believe in a Millennium, but not a literal, earthly one. They argue that the Millennium is the current spiritual reign of Christ over the Church and that it will continue until He returns for His saints. They thus interpret the thousand years as a symbolic period of time.

One appealing aspect of the Amillennial view is its simplicity. The Church Age comes to a screaming halt as a result of the Second Coming. There is no Tribulation, no literal earthly Millennium, and no eternity on a new earth. Augustine spiritualized everything, arguing that the kingdom is the Church, the Millennium is the current Church Age, and the new earth is symbolic language for Heaven.

The Amillennial concept is the majority viewpoint in Christendom today, held by the Catholic Church and most of the old mainline Protestant denominations.

Postmillennialism

The third view of the end times is called Postmillennialism. It is illustrated in figure 3 on page 24. This view did not develop until the mid-17th Century, long after the Reformation. The Reformation had little impact on prophetic views because the Reformation leaders had their attention riveted on the questions of bibli-

cal authority and justification by faith. The Reformers continued to spiritualize prophecy.

The Postmillennial view was a product of the Rationalistic Revolution in thinking. It was developed in the mid-1600's by a Unitarian minister named Daniel Whitby. It was immediately dubbed "Postmillennialism" because it envisioned a return of Jesus after (post) a literal thousand year reign of the Church over all the earth.

Postmillennialism spread quickly within the Protestant world, probably for two reasons. First, it gave Protestants an opportunity to differ from the Catholic position. More importantly, it was a theological expression of the prevailing rationalistic philosophy of the age, a philosophy that boldly proclaimed the ability of Mankind to build the kingdom of heaven on earth.

The Postmillennial view holds that the Church Age will gradually evolve into a "golden age" when the Church will rule over all the world. This will be accomplished through the Christianization of the nations.

To its credit, it can be said that this viewpoint served as a mighty stimulus to missionary efforts during the 18th and 19th Centuries. Missionaries were seized with the vision of speeding up the return of the Lord by preaching the Gospel to all the world.

A Sudden Death

By 1900 nearly all segments of Protestant Christianity had adopted the Postmillennial viewpoint. But the view was to be quickly dropped.

Postmillennialism died almost overnight with the outbreak of the First World War. The reason, of course, is that this great war undermined one of the fundamental assumptions of the Postmillennial viewpoint — the assumption of the inevitability of progress. This had always been a fatal flaw in the Postmillennial concept, due mainly to its birth in Rationalistic Humanism. Its vision of the perfectibility of man and the redemption of society was destroyed by the atrocities of the war.

Another fatal flaw of the Postmillennial viewpoint was its lack of a consistent biblical base. To expound the view, it was necessary to literalize some prophecies (those concerning the Millennium) while at the same time spiritualizing other prophecies (the personal presence of the Lord during the Millennium). Also, it was necessary to ignore or explain away the many prophecies in the Bible that clearly state that society is going to get worse rather than better as the time approaches for the Lord's return (Matthew 24:4-24 and 2 Timothy 3:1-5).

Modern Premillennialism

The modern premillennial viewpoint crystallized in the early 1800's among a group in England known as the Plymouth Brethren. It is illustrated in figure 4 on page 24.

As can be readily seen, this viewpoint revives the historic premillennial view except for its concept of the Rapture of the Church. The Plymouth Brethren envisioned the Second Coming to consist of two stages: first an appearing of Jesus in the heavens for the Church, and second, a return to the earth with His Church. Their concept of the Rapture has since come to be known as the "Pre-Tribulation Rapture" because it contends that the Church will be taken out of the world before the Tribulation begins.

Comparisons

Looking back over these four views of the end times, we can see some significant differences. But let's not overlook the similarities.

- All agree that Jesus is coming back for His saints.
- All agree that the Redeemed will spend eternity in the presence of God.

These two points of agreement are far more important than the many points of disagreement.

Still, the areas of disagreement are significant. Two of the views (the Amillennial and Postmillennial) deny that Jesus will ever manifest His glory before the nations in a worldwide reign of peace, justice and righteousness.

The Postmillennial view also denies the soon coming of the Lord, for according to this view, the Lord cannot return until His Church has ruled over the world for a thousand years.

Likewise, the Historic Premillennial view negates the imminency of the Lord's return, since it combines the Rapture and Second Coming and places them at the end of the Tribulation. In contrast, the Modern Premillennial view allows for the Lord to return at any moment in the Rapture, without the fulfillment of any specific prophecies.

The key to the differences is the approach to Scripture. Again, if you tend to spiritualize Scripture, you will end up with an Amillennial or Postmillennial viewpoint. If you tend to accept Scripture for its plain sense meaning, you will have a Premillennial viewpoint. ❖

Questions:

1) There are many passages in the New Testament that urge us to live watching for the Lord's return (Luke 12:40, Titus 2:11-13, James 5:8-9 and 1 Peter 4:7). This is called "imminency." An imminent event is one that can occur at any moment. Study the charts on page 24 regarding imminency. Which two views allow for the imminent return of the Lord?

_____

2) Fourteen chapters of the book of Revelation (chapters 6-19) are dedicated to a description of Tribulation events. Where is the Tribulation in the Amillennial view? Augustine spiritualized it by arguing that it is just representative of the trials and tribulations we suffer in this life. What do you think?

_____

_____

3) Revelation 20:1-3 says that during the Millennium, Satan will be bound in such a way that he can no longer "deceive the nations." Augustine argued that this occurred at the Cross. Do you believe Satan is bound today in such a way that he is no longer deceiving the nations?

_____

_____

4) The 20th chapter of Revelation says six times that the Millennium will last one thousand years. Augustine's followers believed the Lord would return in 1000 AD. When he did not, they then spiritualized the one thousand years to mean just a "long period of time." What do you think?

_____

_____

5) The Bible says in Revelation 21 that after the Millennium, the Redeemed are going to live eternally in the presence of God on a new earth. Augustine spiritualized the new earth to mean Heaven. Are the Redeemed going to live eternally in Heaven or on the new earth?

_____

_____

6) Why do you think the Plymouth Brethren decided that there had to be a Rapture of the Church before the beginning of the Tribulation?

_____

_____

Lesson 6

Old Testament Prophecy

> **Fact:** *The Old Testament is essential to the understanding of the New Testament and to a comprehension of the Bible's prophetic messages.*

Key Scripture: *"All Scripture is inspired by God and profitable for teaching, for reproof, for correction, for training in righteousness . . ."*(2 Timothy 3:16).

The Problem

It is common today for ministers to focus mainly on the New Testament in their preaching and teaching while hardly citing the Old Testament. Even worse are superficial slogans such as "This is a New Testament church" or "We just preach Jesus."

Yet, in the scripture quotation above, the Apostle Paul emphasized to Timothy that *all* Scripture is profitable. In fact, one verse earlier, Paul stated that "from childhood you [Timothy] have known the sacred writings which are able to give you the wisdom that leads to salvation through faith which is in Christ Jesus." A reader today just assumes that Timothy must have had a copy of the New Testament. But the New Testament did not exist when Paul wrote these words!

Further, Paul admonished Timothy to commit himself to "the public reading of Scripture, to exhortation and teaching" (1 Timothy 4:13). Again, Paul was referring to what we call The Old Testament.

The Importance of the Old Testament

This spiritual malady of ignoring the Old Testament that is epidemic in the Church today is a serious problem because there is no way to understand the New Testament without knowledge of the Old Testament.

For example, Jesus is referred to by Paul in 1 Corinthians 15:20 as the "first fruits" of those to be resurrected. There is no way to understand that expression apart from a knowledge of the Old Testament sacrificial system.

In like manner, Jesus is referred to in the book of Hebrews as the "High Priest of our confession" (Hebrews 3:1) and as "a high priest according to the order of Melchizedek" (Hebrews 5:10). These terms have no meaning apart from a knowledge of the interaction between Abraham and Melchizedek and the role of the High Priest as revealed in the Hebrew Scriptures.

A knowledge of Old Testament prophecy is particularly necessary to the understanding of New Testament prophecy. The books of Daniel and Revelation fit together like a hand in a glove. Neither one can be understood apart from the other.

The book of Revelation contains more than 300 quotes or references to Old Testament passages, and not a single one is identified. A person without knowledge of the Old Testament could read the book of Revelation and never realize how interlaced it is with Old Testament prophecy. Consider the theme of the book that is found in Revelation 1:7 —

> Behold, He is coming with the clouds, and every eye will see Him, even those who pierced Him; and all the tribes of the earth will mourn over Him.

This statement is made up of two quotes from the Old Testament put end-to-end. The first is found in Daniel 7:13 and the second in Zechariah 12:10.

The Gospel in the Old Testament

When Paul told Timothy that the "sacred writings" were sufficient to lead him to salvation through faith in Jesus, he was referring to Old Testament prophecy. The New Testament did not exist at that time.

On the Day of Pentecost following the death, burial and resurrection of Jesus, the Apostle Peter preached the first Gospel sermon in Jerusalem (Acts 2:14-36). From beginning to end, the sermon consisted of quotations of Old Testament prophecies about the Messiah, followed by Peter's declarations that Jesus had fulfilled those prophecies.

Phillip, the evangelist, took the same approach when he met with the Ethiopian eunuch, a devout Jew who had been to Jerusalem to observe the feasts and was returning home to Africa (Acts 8:26-39). Phillip discovered that the man was reading an Old Testament passage from Isaiah about the Messiah coming as a "suffering lamb" (Isaiah 53:1-9).

Phillip explained the passage to the Ethiopian, and the man accepted the fact that Jesus had fulfilled it. In response, he was baptized. He then continued on his way, rejoicing that he had found the Messiah.

The Volume of Prophecy in the Old Testament

The Old Testament contains over 300 specific prophecies about the First Coming of the Messiah. But many of these are repetitious. When those are filtered out, 109 separate and distinct prophecies remain, all of which were fulfilled in the life of Jesus.

The Hebrew Scriptures contain many more prophecies about the Second Coming than the First. And they are scattered throughout, from Genesis to Malachi. People normally think of only the Major and Minor Prophets, but the Psalms are full of prophecy, like Psalm 22, which prophesies about the crucifixion of the Messiah in detail, written one thousand years before the birth of Jesus.

Even the historical books of the Old Testament contain prophecies. The very first Messianic prophecy in the Bible is found in Genesis 3:15. It states that the Messiah will be born of a virgin. Deuteronomy 31 prophesies that if the Jewish people are unfaithful to God they will be dispersed among the nations of the world and be persecuted wherever they go.

The Second Coming in Old Testament Prophecy

The Bible teaches that Jesus will

establish His personal reign over all the earth at the time of His Second Coming, and the Old Testament contains many prophecies about that event. As we have already seen, Zechariah 14 says the Lord will return to the Mount of Olives from which He ascended into Heaven and at that time, He will become "king over all the earth" (Zechariah 14:9).

In Isaiah's account of the same event, he refers to the Lord returning to Mount Zion, which is an alternative name for Jerusalem: "So will the Lord of hosts come down to wage war on Mount Zion and on its hill. Like flying birds, so the Lord of hosts will protect Jerusalem. He will protect and rescue it; He will pass over and rescue it" (Isaiah 31:4b-5).

Both Isaiah and Jeremiah portray the Lord returning in wrath. Jeremiah says He will "roar" from the heavens (Jeremiah 25:30-31). Isaiah says He will be "filled with indignation" and His tongue will be like "a consuming fire" (Isaiah 30:27-28). Zephaniah says the day of His return will be one of "trouble and distress" and "destruction and desolation" (Zephaniah 1:14-18).

The Millennium in the Old Testament

Once the Messiah has poured out the wrath of God on the enemies of God, He will establish His reign over the earth, and He will begin to manifest His glory: "Then the moon will be abashed and the sun ashamed, for the Lord of hosts will reign on Mount Zion and in Jerusalem, and His glory will be before His elders" (Isaiah 24:23).

All the various aspects about the Lord's millennial reign are spelled out in detail in the book of Isaiah.

The book of Revelation is about the Tribulation. It is the book of Isaiah that reveals the details of the Millennium. The only new information about the Millennium contained in the book of Revelation is that it will last one thousand years (Revelation 20:2-7).

Foundational Truths

The Old Testament presents the framework for understanding the meaning of life and God's purposes in history. It provides the answers to some of our most fundamental questions:

- Where did the creation come from?
- What is the purpose of life?
- Why is there pain and suffering and death in the world?
- Why does Mankind need a Savior?

The Attitude of Jesus

Jesus had great respect for the Hebrew Scriptures. He quoted them in response to the temptations of Satan (Matthew 4:1-11). He quoted them in His Sermon on the Mount as he laid down guidelines for Christian living (Matthew 5). He quoted the book of Daniel in His last discourse to His disciples (Matthew 24:15). He referenced the book of Jonah when teaching about His death, burial and resurrection (Matthew 12:40).

And shortly before His ascension into Heaven, Jesus told His disciples: "These are My words which I spoke to you while I was still with you, that all things which are written about Me in the Law of Moses and the Prophets and the Psalms must be fulfilled" (Luke 24:44).

A Tragedy

The Old Testament has been terribly abused in modern history by theologians who are determined to reconcile it to science (meaning the theories of Evolution). Thus, they have spiritualized the first few chapters of Genesis to mean anything but what they say.

The six days of creation have been transformed into six billion years, and Adam and Eve have become mythical or symbolic creatures, not real human beings. And in like manner, the worldwide flood of Noah's time has been converted into a regional flood confined to a small area of the Middle East.

These efforts have undermined the integrity of the Scriptures. The result is that for many people, the Old Testament has become a book of fairy tales.

This raises a very serious issue: if we cannot believe the beginning of the Bible, how can we believe any of it? If God did not create the universe in six literal days, as Genesis clearly teaches, then how do we know for certain that the Bible is correct when it says that Jesus was resurrected from the dead or when it says that one day Jesus will return to this earth to reign?

It is no accident that those who spiritualize the beginning of the Bible are also those who spiritualize the ending, claiming Jesus is never going to return to reign over all the earth.

A Plea

We need to take the Scriptures seriously — all of them, both the Old and New Testaments. We need to stop playing games with them in order to placate the claims of science and the desires of our hearts.

Take the time to read Psalm 119. It is the longest of the psalms, with a total of 176 verses. The theme is found in verse 105: "Your word is a lamp to my feet and a light to my path." Accordingly, almost every verse of this psalm mentions the Word of God in one way or another.

The sum of Your word is truth, and every one of Your righteous ordinances is everlasting.
(Psalm 119: 160) ✤

Quotations

"Bible prophecy was given to show and to reveal — not to puzzle and veil." — Paul Lee Tan, *The Interpretation of Prophecy* (Assurance Publishers, 1974).

"I believe God knows how to communicate. I believe He says what He means and means what He says. I don't believe you have to have a doctorate in hermeneutics to understand the Bible. The essentials, instead, are an honest heart and the in-dwelling of God's Spirit (1 Corinthians 2:10-16)." — David R. Reagan, *God's Plan for the Ages: The Blueprint of Bible Prophecy* (Lamb & Lion Ministries, 2005).

Questions:

1) What is your favorite Old Testament book, and why?

_____

_____

2) What is your least favorite Old Testament book, and why?

_____

_____

3) Read Isaiah 11:4-9. What is your interpretation of this passage?

_____

_____

4) Read Isaiah 11:10-12. What do you think this passage means?

_____

_____

5) Read Isaiah 59:15b-19. Do you see both the First and Second Comings in this passage?

_____

_____

6) What prophetic implications do you see in Psalms 47 and 48, if any?

_____

_____

_____

7) Read Ezekiel 37:1-12. Many theologians contend that this is a prophecy about the Church. What do you think, and why?

_____

_____

_____

8) Read Zechariah 14:1-9. What do you think is the meaning of this passage?

_____

_____

Jesus in the Old Testament

Genesis	– The Seed of Woman who will one day crush Satan.
Exodus	– The Passover Lamb who will be sacrificed for our sins.
Leviticus	– Our High Priest before God's throne.
Numbers	– Our Heavenly Guide.
Deuteronomy	– The Great Prophet to come, prophesied by Moses.
Joshua	– Our Captain of Salvation.
Judges	– Our Judge and Law Giver.
Ruth	– Our Kinsman Redeemer.
1 & 2 Samuel	– Our Trusted Prophet.
Kings and Chronicles	– Our Righteous Ruler.
Ezra	– Our Great Teacher.
Nehemiah	– Our Restorer.
Esther	– Our Advocate.
Job	– Our Redeemer.
Psalms	– Our Shepherd.
Proverbs	– Our Wisdom.
Ecclesiastes	– Our Ultimate Judge.
Song of Solomon	– Our Loving Bridegroom.
Isaiah	– Our Suffering Servant.
Jeremiah	– Our Compassionate Judge.
Lamentations	– Our Consoler.
Ezekiel	– The Lord of Nations.
Daniel	– The Son of Man.
Hosea	– The Faithful Husband.
Joel	– The Holy Spirit Baptizer.
Amos	– The Lord of Justice.
Obadiah	– The Coming King.
Jonah	– The Forgiving One.
Micah	– The Lord of Righteousness.
Nahum	– The Avenger.
Habakkuk	– The Watchman.
Zephaniah	– The Lord of Wrath.
Haggai	– The Lord of Hosts.
Zachariah	– The Humble King.
Malachi	– The Son of Righteousness.

"You search the Scriptures because you think that in them you have eternal life; it is these that testify about Me" (John 5:39).

Lesson 7

Messianic Prophecy

> **Fact:** *There are 109 separate and distinct prophecies in the Old Testament regarding the First Coming of the Messiah.*

Key Scripture: *"But from you, Bethlehem Ephrathah . . . from you One will go forth for Me to be ruler in Israel. His goings forth are from long ago, from the days of eternity"* (Micah 5:2)

The Quantity
of Messianic Prophecy

Most scholars agree that there are about 300 prophecies in the Old Testament that relate to the First Coming of the Messiah. But, these are not 300 different prophecies. Many, like the prophecy that the Messiah will be born of the seed of Abraham, are repeated several times.

When all the repetitive prophecies are culled out, there remain slightly more than one hundred distinctively different, specific prophecies about the Messiah's First Advent.

There are also many First Coming prophecies in the New Testament Gospels. An overview of these are presented in chapter 11.

Old Testament Prophecies

In the outline that follows, a sampling is given of the 109 Old Testament specific prophecies about the First Advent. They are classified into categories related to the chronology of the life of Christ. In each case

the prophecy's origin is cited from a major Old Testament source, followed by a reference to the New Testament fulfillment.

One interesting thing to note is that most of the 34 prophecies regarding the Messiah's death were all fulfilled in a 24 hour period.

The Messiah's Lineage:

- From the Shemite branch of humanity – Genesis 9:26 / Luke 3:36

- Through Abraham – Genesis 12:3 / Matthew 1:1

- Through Abraham's son, Isaac – Genesis 17:21 / Luke 3:34

- Through the tribe of Judah – Genesis 49:8 / Luke 3:33-34

- Through the family of Jesse – Isaiah 11:1 / Matthew 1:6

- Through the house of David – Jeremiah 23:5 / Luke 3:31-32

The Messiah's Birth & Childhood:

- Place of the birth – Micah 5:2 / Matthew 2:1

- A star will signal the birth – Numbers 24:17 / Matthew 2:2

- Born of a virgin – Isaiah 7:14 / Luke 1:34-35

- Presented with gifts at birth –

Psalm 72:10-11 / Matthew 2:1,11

- Infants of Bethlehem to be massacred – Jeremiah 31:15 / Matt. 2:16

- Sojourn in Egypt – Hosea 11:1 / Matthew 2:14-15

Messiah's Life and Ministry

- Spirit-filled and anointed from birth – Isa. 11:1-2 / Luke 2:46-47

- Preceded by a prophet who would prepare His way – Isaiah 40:3 / Matthew 3:1-3

- Do battle with Satan – Genesis 3:15 / Matthew 4:1

- Ministry centered in Galilee – Isaiah 9:1 / Matthew 4:13

- Prophet – Deuteronomy 18:15,18 / Matthew 21: 11

- Miracle Worker – Isaiah 11:2 / John 3:2

- Humble in Spirit – Zechariah 9:9 / Philippians 2:8

- Preach the Gospel to the poor – Isaiah 61:1 / Matthew 11:4-5

- Heal the sick – Isaiah 53:4-5 / Matthew 8:16-17

- Rejected by the Jews – Psalm 69:7-8 / John 1:11

- Accepted by the Gentiles – Hosea 2:23 / Acts 28:28

Messiah's Nature

- Eternal – Micah 5:2 / John 1:1,14

- Divine – Isaiah 9:6 / John 10:30

- Human – Psalm 8:5 / John 1:14

- Son of God – Psa. 2:7 / Matt. 3:17

- A sacrificial lamb – Isaiah 53:7 / John 1:29

- A sin bearer – Isaiah 53:4-6 / 1 Peter 2:24

Messiah's Death

- Entry into Jerusalem on a donkey – Zechariah 9:9 / John 12:12-15

- Betrayal by a friend – Psalm 41:9 / Matthew 26:20-21

- Betrayed for 30 pieces of silver – Zech. 11:12 / Matthew 26:14-15

- Forsaken by His disciples – Zechariah 13:7 / Matthew 26:55-56

- Scourged – Isa. 50:6 / Matt. 27:26

- Death by crucifixion – Psalm 22:16 / Luke 23:33

- Darkness at noon – Amos 8:9 / Matthew 27:45

- A cry of victory – Psalm 22:31 / John 19:30

- Buried in a rich man's tomb – Isaiah 53:9 / Matthew 27:57-60

Messiah's Resurrection and Ascension

- Resurrection – Psalm 16:10 / Mark 16:6

- Ascension – Psa. 68:18 / Acts 1:9

- Exaltation at the right hand of God – Psalm 110:1 / Mark 16:19

Amazing Fulfillment

Now, these are only 41 of the 109 prophecies about the Messiah, all of which were fulfilled in the life of Jesus.

The absolutely amazing fulfillment of Messianic prophecy in the life of Jesus was illustrated brilliantly back in the 1950s by a California professor of mathematics and astronomy named Peter Stoner.

Stoner selected eight of the best known prophecies about the Messiah and calculated the odds of their accidental fulfillment in one person as being 1 in 10^{17}.

Stoner illustrated the meaning of this number by asking people to imagine filling the State of Texas knee deep in silver dollars, with one of those coins having a black check mark on it. Then, turn a blindfolded person loose in this sea of silver dollars. The odds that the first coin he would pick up would be the one with the black check mark are the same as eight prophecies being fulfilled accidentally in the life of Jesus.

The fulfillment of all these prophecies in the life of Jesus is proof that He was who He said He was — namely, God in the flesh. They are also proof that the Bible is the Word of God.

A Great Messianic Passage

One of the most important Messianic passages in the Old Testament is Isaiah 53.

It prophesies that the Messiah will be a "man of sorrows" and a "lamb that is led to slaughter." He will be "pierced through for our transgressions" and "crushed for our iniquities." He will be a "guilt offering" in our behalf. He will die with wicked men, but his grave will come from a rich man. And despite His death, He will live again to "see His offspring." In summary, He will "pour out Himself to death in order to "justify the many," both Jew and Gentile who place their faith in Him. ✤

Questions:

1) Jewish rabbis argue that Isaiah 53 describes the nation of Israel, not the Messiah. Read the passage. What do you think?

2) What do you think of Peter Stoner's calculations. Do you find them convincing?

3) Read Psalm 22. Notice that from the beginning to the end, it is a prophecy about the crucifixion of the Messiah. See how many prophecies about the Messiah's death you can find in this passage.

4) Some argue that Jesus consciously fulfilled the prophecies, pointing to Matthew 21:1-7. But if He had been merely a human, could He have fulfilled all of them on purpose — like choosing the place of His birth or the method of His death?

5) The very first Messianic prophecy in the Scriptures is recorded in Genesis 3:15. It is not easy to understand because it is expressed in symbolic language. What do you think it means?

Lesson 8

Two Cornerstone Prophecies

> **Fact:** *The Book of Daniel contains two key prophecies that present an overview from his time to the Second Coming of the Messiah.*

Key Scripture: *"He* [Jesus in a pre-incarnate appearance] *said to me, 'O Daniel, man of high esteem, understand the words that I am about to tell you and stand upright, for I have now been sent to you.' And when He had spoken this word to me, I stood up trembling"* (Daniel 10:11).

A Man of High Esteem

Daniel is referred to in the Hebrew Scriptures as one of the most righteous men who had ever lived, together with Noah and Job (Ezekiel 14:14). In the passage quoted above, he is told that God held him in "high esteem."

It was to this man that God gave two of the most important prophecies recorded in the Old Testament. One is "The Prophecy of the Kingdoms" which is recorded in Daniel 2:31-45. The other is usually referred to as "The Prophecy of the 70 Weeks of Years." It can be found in Daniel 9:24-27.

These are foundational prophecies because each one presents an overview of events from the time of Daniel to the Second Coming of the Messiah. And The Prophecy of the 70 Weeks of Years also provides the timing of the Lord's First Coming. So, let's take a brief look at these two prophecies.

The Prophecy of the Kingdoms

Early in the 70 years of the Jew's Babylonian captivity, in about 603 BC, the king of Babylon, Nebuchadnezzar, had a dream that deeply disturbed him (Daniel 2:1-16). When his wise men could not help him remember the dream nor give him an interpretation, one of the Jewish captives, a young man named Daniel, sent word to the king that through the power of his God, he could both reveal the dream and give its interpretation (Daniel 2:17-30).

Daniel told the king that he had seen in his dream a great and splendid statue. The head was made of gold, the arms and chest of silver, the thighs of bronze and the legs of iron. Its feet were composed of an unstable mixture of iron and clay. (See the diagram on page 40.) As the king was admiring the statue, a supernatural stone suddenly crushed the feet, turning the whole statue into a pile of dust. The stone then expanded into a mountain that filled the whole earth (Daniel 2:31-35).

Daniel proceeded to give the interpretation of the dream. He told Nebuchadnezzar that the head of gold represented the Babylonian Empire, the chest of silver was the Medo-Persian Empire and the thighs of bronze were symbolic of the Greek Empire that would conquer the Medes and Persians (Daniel 2:36-40 and 8:20-21). Daniel did not specifically identify the fourth kingdom symbolized by the legs of iron, but we know from history that it was the Roman Empire, with the legs representing the Western and Eastern manifestations of the empire.

We know from other prophecies about the end times that the fragile feet represented the last Gentile empire of history — namely, the worldwide empire of the Antichrist which would appear very powerful on the outside but would be rotten within — thus the symbol of iron mixed with clay (Daniel 2:41-46).

The supernatural stone, "cut out without hands," represented the kingdom of the Messiah. Its crushing of the statue was a prophecy that at the Second Coming of the Messiah, His kingdom will supplant all the Gentile kingdoms of the world and will encompass the entire earth (Daniel 2: 45).

Fifty years later, this same sequence of empires was presented to Daniel in a vision, but instead of a glorious statue, Daniel saw a series of devouring wild beasts — representing the way God views the kingdoms of Man (Daniel 8:1-13, 20-27).

Those who do not believe Jesus will ever return to this earth to reign argue that the supernatural stone that takes over the world represents the Church. But that cannot be true because the New Testament never pictures the Church taking over the world. In fact, the end time prophecies about the Church indicate that it will become increasingly weak because of heresies and apostasy. Further, Daniel is told several times that the prophecies given to him pertain to the end times (Daniel 8:19, 10:14 and 12:4,9).

The 70 Weeks of Years

Twenty-five years after Daniel revealed and interpreted Nebuchadnezzar's dream of the sequence of world empires, he was given a sweeping overview prophecy about the future which has come to be known as "The Prophecy of the 70 Weeks of Years" — representing a period of 490 years (Daniel 9:24-27 – see the diagram on page 41).

The prophecy was given to Daniel by the Angel Gabriel (Daniel 9:20-23). Daniel was told that God was going to accomplish six goals among the Jewish people during a period of 490 years. The goals were (Daniel 9:24):

1) "Finish the transgression" (end the rebellion of the Jewish people against their Messiah).

2) "Make an end of sin" (by bringing the Jewish people to repentance and the acceptance of their Messiah).

3) "Make atonement for iniquity" (through the sacrifice of the Messiah).

4) "Bring in everlasting righteousness" (with the establishment of the Messianic Kingdom).

5) "Seal up vision and prophecy" (through the fulfillment of all Messianic prophecies).

6) "Anoint a most holy place" (through provision of the Millennial Temple described in Ezekiel 40-46 and the return of God's Shekinah Glory to it as described in Ezekiel 43:1-2).

Daniel was told that the 490 years would begin with the "issuing of a decree to restore and rebuild Jerusalem" (Daniel 9:25). It was then revealed that 69 weeks of years thereafter (483 years) the Messiah would come and be "cut off" (Daniel 9:26). That would be followed by the Temple being destroyed (Daniel 9:26). The final week of years (7 years) would take place after "the prince who is to come" (the Antichrist) makes a "firm covenant" with Israel (Daniel 9:27).

This is an amazing prophecy. For one thing, it pinpoints the time of the First Coming of the Messiah. Scholars disagree over the starting point of the prophecy in history. There are three possible dates, but regardless of which date you use, the 483 years leading up to the cutting off (killing) of the Messiah concludes either during the ministry of Jesus or on the very day He entered Jerusalem for the last time.

This, incidentally, is an immense problem for the Jewish people since it means, according to one of their own prophets, that the Messiah had to come before 70 A.D. when the Temple was destroyed by the Romans.

Those who do not believe in a future reign of Jesus here on earth try to argue that the final seven years of the prophecy occurred immediately following His crucifixion. But this cannot be true because only one of the six goals to be accomplished among the Jewish people during the 490 years of the prophecy has yet become a reality — and that is the atonement for sins. The other five goals remain unaccomplished.

So, the prophecy must have a gap between the 483 years and the final seven years. And that gap, of course, is the current Church Age. The final seven years will not start until the Antichrist signs a covenant with Israel. That will launch the seven year period of the Tribulation that is described in detail in the book of Revelation. During that time the Jewish people will be brought to the end of themselves, motivating them to repent and receive Yeshua (Jesus) as their Messiah (Zechariah 12:10 and Matthew 23:39).

Regarding the gap, think of it this way: there are four quarters of 15 minutes each in a football game, for a total of one hour. But most football games last more than three hours. Why? Because of gaps called "time outs" and a half time break. We are currently in a time out of the 70 Weeks of Years prophecy. It will end when the Antichrist makes his covenant with Israel. ✥

Quotation:

"There is not a liberal theologian in the world, past or present, who accepts the authenticity of the Book of Daniel. They all deny its integrity, declaring the book to be a blatant, patent forgery. They define its contents as pure, unadulterated fiction . . . We ask: Why this increasing and vicious attack against the book? The answer is clear and plain. The book is discredited because of the attempt on the part of modern rationalism to destroy the supernatural and the prophetic in the Bible. The ultimate aim of the destructive critic is to make of the Bible a human book like any other book." — W. A. Criswell (1909-2002), pastor of First Baptist in Dallas, TX.

Nebuchadnezzar's Dream

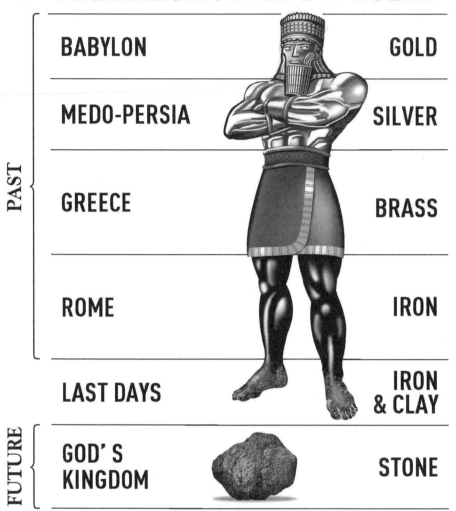

PAST		
BABYLON		GOLD
MEDO-PERSIA		SILVER
GREECE		BRASS
ROME		IRON
LAST DAYS		IRON & CLAY

FUTURE		
GOD'S KINGDOM		STONE

(Illustration by Stephen Cymerman)

DANIEL'S SEVENTY WEEKS (Daniel 9:24-27)

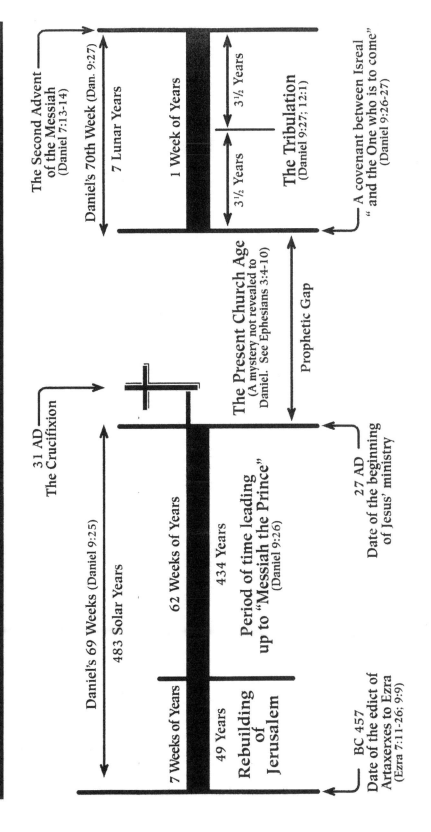

The Second Advent of the Messiah (Daniel 7:13-14)

Daniel's 70th Week (Dan. 9:27)

7 Lunar Years

1 Week of Years

3½ Years

3½ Years

The Tribulation (Daniel 9:27; 12:1)

A covenant between Isreal "and the One who is to come" (Daniel 9:26-27)

The Present Church Age (A mystery not revealed to Daniel. See Ephesians 3:4-10)

Prophetic Gap

31 AD The Crucifixion

27 AD Date of the beginning of Jesus' ministry

Daniel's 69 Weeks (Daniel 9:25)

483 Solar Years

62 Weeks of Years

434 Years

Period of time leading up to "Messiah the Prince" (Daniel 9:26)

7 Weeks of Years

49 Years Rebuilding of Jerusalem

BC 457 Date of the edict of Artaxerxes to Ezra (Ezra 7:11-26; 9:9)

Questions:

1) What have your learned from these two cornerstone prophecies taken from the book of Daniel?

_____

_____

_____

2) Read Daniel 12: 8-9, and you will see that Daniel did not fully understand these prophecies when they were given to him. He was told not to worry about it because the prophecies would be understood when the time came for them to be fulfilled. There are many prophecies like this in the Bible — prophecies that depend on either historical or technological developments to be understood. For example, read Revelation 11:3-13. What is it about this prophecy that made it impossible to understand in natural terms before the mid-1960s?

_____

_____

3) Liberals hate the book of Daniel because they do not believe in supernatural revelation. They try to argue that the book was written around the time of Jesus, and therefore they claim it is a fraudulent book in which another author wrote history as if he were prophesying it. Read Matthew 24:15-21, and then read Daniel 9:27, 11:31 and 12:11. Do you think Jesus' quotation of Daniel validates the book?

_____

_____

4) Those who do not believe that Jesus will ever return to reign on this earth have a hard time explaining away Daniel's vision in chapter 7. Read Daniel 7:13-14,18 and 27. What do you think?

_____

_____

5) Did you notice that The Prophecy of the 70 Weeks of Years identifies the timing of both the First and Second Comings of Jesus? Study the prophecy and see if you can determine where it makes these identifications.

_____

_____

_____

Lesson 9

The Jews in Prophecy

> **Fact:** *The Bible's prophetic focus on Israel is second only to its prophecies concerning the Messiah.*

Key Scripture: *"For you* [the Jewish people] *are a holy people to the LORD your God, and the LORD has chosen you to be a people for His own possession out of all the peoples who are on the face of the earth"* (Deuteronomy 14:2).

God's Chosen People

The Jewish people are the Chosen People of God eternally. That does not mean they are saved. It means that God selected them to be a witness of Him to the world. And thus, it was through them that God gave the Scriptures and provided the Messiah.

They also serve as a witness of what it means to have a relationship with God. Accordingly, their history shows that when you are faithful to God and His Word, He blesses, and when you are unfaithful, He disciplines. But their history also demonstrates that when you repent, God forgives and forgets and begins to bless again.

This is true even to this day. The Jewish people are currently under discipline because of their rejection of Jesus as their Messiah, but Bible prophecy makes it clear that a great remnant of them are going to come to salvation in the end times by accepting Jesus as their Messiah (Zechariah 12:10).

Prophecies Fulfilled

The Hebrew Scriptures are full of prophecies about the Jewish people. Many of the prophecies were fulfilled in Old Testaments times. These include prophecies that the northern nation of Israel would be destroyed by the Assyrians (Isaiah 8:1-10), and the southern nation of Judah would be taken into captivity by the Babylonians (Isaiah 39:6). Jeremiah also prophesied that the Babylonian captivity would last exactly 70 years (Jeremiah 25:8-12).

Throughout Old Testament times, significant prophecies were given to Jewish kings. The prophet Micaiah warned Ahab and Jehoshaphat that they would be defeated in battle (2 Chronicles 18:12-17). Isaiah assured King Hezekiah that Jerusalem would not fall to the Assyrians (Isaiah 37:6-7). The prophet Nathan told King David that because of his sin with Bathsheba, their baby would die and David would suffer rebellion within his own family (2 Samuel 12:7-15).

End Time Prophecies

Prophecies regarding the Jewish people in the end times can be found throughout the Hebrew Scriptures and the New Testament. Four of them were fulfilled before the beginning of the 20th Century.

1) Dispersion — The Jews were

warned repeatedly that they would be dispersed worldwide if they were not faithful to their covenant with God. Consider the words of Moses: "The Lord will scatter you among all peoples, from one end of the earth to the other . . ." (Deuteronomy 28:64; see also Leviticus 26:33).

2) **Persecution** — The Lord also warned the Jews that they would be persecuted wherever they were dispersed. Again, the words of Moses are graphic in this regard: "Among those nations you shall find no rest, and there shall be no resting place for the sole of your foot; but there the Lord will give you a trembling heart, failing of eyes, and despair of soul" (Deuteronomy 28:65).

3) **Desolation** — God promised that after their dispersion, their land would become "desolate" and their cities would become "waste" (Leviticus 26:33). Moses put it more graphically when he said, "the foreigner who comes from a distant land . . will say, 'All its land is brimstone and salt, a burning waste, unsown and unproductive, and no grass grows in it'" (Deuteronomy 29:22-23).

4) **Preservation** — But God in His marvelous grace promised He would preserve the Jews as a separate people during their worldwide wanderings. (See Isaiah 66:22, Jeremiah 30:11 and Jeremiah 31:35-37.) Isaiah puts it in a colorful way. He says the Lord could no more forget Israel than a mother could forget her nursing child (Isaiah 49:15). He then adds that God cannot forget Israel because He has them tattooed on the palms of His hands (Isaiah 49:16)!

Fulfillment

God has fulfilled all four of these prophecies during the past 2,000 years. In 70 A.D. the Romans destroyed the city of Jerusalem and took the Jewish nation into captivity, desolating the land and scattering the Jewish people across the face of the earth. As prophesied, everywhere the Jews went they were persecuted, with their persecution culminating in the Nazi Holocaust of World War II.

But God also preserved the Jews, and the fulfillment of this prophecy has been one of the most remarkable miracles of history. No other people have ever been so dispersed and yet been able to retain their identity as a nation.

Current Prophecies

We are privileged to live in an age when God is fulfilling many prophecies regarding the Jews. What a testimony this is to the fact that God is alive and well, that God is on His throne and in control, and that God is faithful to His promises.

1) **Regathering of the People** — The Old Testament prophets promised repeatedly that the day would come when God would regather the Jews to the land of Israel (see Isaiah 11:10-12 and Ezekiel 36:22-28). This remarkable regathering of the Jews from the four corners of the earth has occurred in our life time. World War I prepared the land for the people as the control of Palestine was transferred from a nation that hated the Jews (the Turks) to a nation that was sympathetic to their return (Britain). The Holocaust of World War II prepared the people for the land by motivating them to return.

2) **Re-establishment of the State** — The prophets stated that when the people were regathered, the nation of Israel would be re-established (see Isaiah 66:7-8 and Zechariah 12:3-6).

This occurred on May 14, 1948. This is the cornerstone prophetic event of our age. It is an event that prophetic scholars have pointed to for 400 years amid much scoffing and ridicule by those who did not believe that Israel would ever exist again as a nation.

3) Reclamation of the Land — God promised that with the re-establishment of the nation, the land would bloom again (Isaiah 35:1-7 and Joel 2:21-26). As Ezekiel put it, people would one day exclaim: "This desolate land has become like the garden of Eden!" (Ezekiel 36:35). And that is exactly what people exclaim today when they visit Israel, for it is once again a land of milk and honey. Over 200 million trees were planted during the 20th Century. Rainfall during that century increased 450 percent. The former malaria infested swamps have been converted into cultivated land. Water from the Sea of Galilee has been channeled to the deserts, causing them to bloom.

4) Revival of the Language — When the Jews were scattered worldwide in the First Century, they ceased speaking the Hebrew language. The Jews who settled in Europe developed a language called Yiddish (a combination of Hebrew and German). The Jews in the Mediterranean basin mixed Hebrew with Spanish to produce a language called Ladino. The prophet Zephaniah implied a time would come when the Hebrew language would be revived (Zephaniah 3:9). It has been. Today the Israelis speak biblical Hebrew. It is the only example in history of the resurrection of a dead language. The man God used to revive the language was Eliezer Ben Yehuda (1858-1922).

5) Re-occupation of Jerusalem — Jesus said that one of the surest signs of His imminent return would be the re-occupation of Jerusalem by the Jews (Luke 21:24). This occurred during the Six Day War in June 1967.

6) Resurgence of Military Strength — Zechariah prophesied that when the Jews were re-established in the land, their military strength would be overwhelming — like "a flaming torch among sheaves" — and that they would "consume" all the peoples around them (Zechariah 12:6). Need anything be said about the fulfillment of this prophecy?

7) Re-focusing of World Politics — Israel is always pictured as the focal point of world politics in the end times (Zechariah 12:3 and 14:1-9). This has been true since the Arab oil boycott in 1973. The West suddenly realized its dependence on Arab oil and began to line up behind the Arab obsession to annihilate Israel.

Future Prophecies

As we witness ancient promises to the Jewish people being fulfilled before our eyes today, we can be assured that God will one day fulfill all the remaining prophecies concerning the fate of Israel.

1) Tribulation — God will put the Jewish people through an unparalleled period of tribulation (Deuteronomy 4:30), during which two-thirds of the Jews will perish (Zechariah 13:8-9). The purpose will be to soften the hearts of a remnant so that they will accept Jesus as their Messiah.

2) Salvation — At the end of the Tribulation, a remnant of the Jews will "look upon Him whom they have pierced" and will accept Him as Lord and Savior (Zechariah 12:10 and Romans 11:1-6, 25-29). On that glorious day, the Bible says "a fountain of salvation will be opened for the house of David and the inhabitants of Jerusalem, for sin and for impurity" (Zechariah 13:1).

3) Primacy — At the Second Coming of Jesus, God will regather all the believing Jews to Israel where they will be established as the prime nation in the world during the Millennium. (See Deuteronomy 28:1,13, 2 Samuel 7:9. Isaiah 60-62 and Micah 4:1-7.) God's blessings to the world will once again flow through the Jewish people, and thus, when a Jew walks by, ten Gentiles will grab his robe and say, "Let us go with you for we have heard that God is with you" (Zechariah 8:23). ✤

Questions:

1) Do you think the modern day fulfillment of so many prophecies regarding the Jewish people is an indication that we are living in the season of the Lord's return?

_____

2) One of the oldest prophecies in the Bible regarding the Jewish people is contained in a speech by Moses found in Deuteronomy 4:27-31. Read this prophecy and give your interpretation of "distress . . . in the latter days."

_____

_____

3) Read Ezekiel 44:1-3, and then Google "Eastern Gate of Jerusalem" on the Internet. Would you say the history of this gate fulfills this prophecy?

_____

_____

4) There is a very interesting symbolic prophecy about the Jewish people in Isaiah 66:7-8. What do you think it means?

_____

_____

5) Read Zechariah 8:1-8. What do you think this passage is talking about?

_____

_____

6) Did you know that Jesus prophesied that He would not return to this earth until the Jewish people accept Him as their Messiah? See Matthew 23:37-39. When do you think this will happen?

_____

Lesson 10

Replacement Theology

> **Fact:** *Many Christians believe the Church has replaced Israel, and God has washed His hands of the Jews.*

Key Scripture: *"Then what advantage has the Jew? Or what is the benefit of circumcision? Great in every respect. First of all, that they were entrusted with the oracles of God. What then? If some did not believe, their unbelief will not nullify the faithfulness of God, will it? May it never be! Rather, let God be found true, though every man be found a liar . . ."* (Romans 3:1-4).

Early History

Very early in the history of the Church a pernicious doctrine began to develop that demonized the Jewish people and argued that they should be persecuted for rejecting Jesus as their Messiah. This is ironic when you consider the fact that the Church began as a Jewish institution. It was founded in Judea by Jews who were followers of a Jewish Messiah, and all its founding documents were written by Jews.

But the distinctive Jewish flavor of early Christianity was not to last long. As the Church began to spread beyond Judea, its message was embraced by more and more Gentiles who had no interest in maintaining contact with the Church's Jewish roots. Even worse, the new Gentile leaders began to turn against the Jews by characterizing them as "Christ killers."

Consider the following examples:

Ignatius of Antioch (ca 50-117 A.D.) — Taught that those who partake of the Passover are partakers with those who killed Jesus.

Justin Martyr (100-106 A.D.) — Claimed God's covenant with Israel was no longer valid and that the Gentiles had replaced the Jews.

Irenaeus (ca 130-202 A.D.) — Declared the Jews were disinherited from the grace of God.

Tertullian (ca 155-230 A.D.) — Blamed the Jews for the death of Jesus and argued they had been rejected by God.

Eusebius (ca 275-339 A.D.) — Taught that the promises of Scripture were meant for the Gentiles and the curses were meant for the Jews and he asserted that the Church was the "true Israel."

John Chrysostom (349-407 A.D.) — Preached a series of sermons against the Jews in which he stated, "The synagogue is not only a brothel and a theater, it is also a den of robbers and lodging place for wild beasts . . . Jews are inveterate murderers possessed by the Devil. Their debauchery and drunkenness gives the manners of a pig." He denied that Jews could ever receive forgiveness. He claimed it was a Christian duty to hate Jews. He claimed that Jews worshiped Satan. And this man was canonized a saint!

Jerome (ca 347-420 A.D.) — Described the Jews as ". . . serpents wearing the image of Judas. Their psalms and prayers are the braying of donkeys . . . They are incapable of understanding Scripture . . ."

St. Augustine (354-430 A.D.) — Asserted that the Jews deserved death but were destined to wander the earth to witness the victory of the Church over the synagogue."

The Middle Ages
(5th to 15th Centuries)

By the Middle Ages, two erroneous concepts had become established Church doctrine:

1) The Jews should be considered "Christ killers" and should be mistreated accordingly.

2) The Church has replaced Israel, and God has no future purpose for the Jews.

These concepts were reinforced throughout the Middle Ages through the Crusades, the Inquisition, passion plays and blood libels. The Jews were even blamed for the Black Plague epidemic.

The Reformation
(1517-1648)

Unfortunately, the Reformation produced no changes in attitude. In fact, the hatred of the Jews was reinforced and intensified by the writings of Martin Luther, the very man who launched the Reformation.

Initially, Luther was sympathetic toward the Jews because he believed their rejection of the Gospel was due to their recognition of the corruption of the Roman Catholic Church. But when they continued to reject the Gospel, Luther turned on them with a vengeance. In 1543 he wrote a pamphlet entitled "Concerning The Jews and Their Lies." The document was an anti-Semitic diatribe. In it, he referred to the Jews as: "A miserable and accursed people," "stupid fools," "miserable, blind and senseless," "thieves and robbers" and "the great vermin of humanity."

Having dehumanized and demonized them, Luther then proceeded to make some startling proposals for dealing with them. He advocated that their synagogues and schools be burned, their houses be destroyed, and their sacred writings be confiscated. He further called for their money to be taken from them and they be compelled into forced labor.

Needless to say, the Nazis gleefully quoted Luther as they rose to power and launched the Holocaust. In his book *Mein Kampf*, published in 1925, Adolf Hitler referred to Martin Luther as "a great warrior, a true statesmen, and a great reformer."

The Attitude Today

The horror of the Holocaust tended to mute the most radical forms of anti-Semitism among Christian leaders. But in reality, anti-Semitism continues today in a new sophisticated form called anti-Zionism. Whereas anti-Semitism sought to drive out the Jews from the lands where they lived, anti-Zionism refuses to accept their right to live in their own land.

The anti-Zionists continue to argue that the Church has replaced Israel and God has abrogated all his promises to the Jewish people, including their claim to the land of Israel.

The Biblical View

The idea that the Church ever replaced Israel is not rooted in the Bible. Rather, it is an expression of irrational anti-Semitism. That does not mean that all who believe in Replacement Theology are anti-Semitic. Most believe it because it is what they have been taught, and they have no idea where the concept came from and the damage it has done to the Jewish people.

Go back and read the verses from Romans 3 that are quoted at the beginning of this chapter. Paul asks if God has rejected the Jewish people because of their unbelief. For almost 2,000 years the Church has shouted, "Yes!" But what does Paul say in response to his question? "May it never be!" He makes the same point again in Romans 11. He begins that chapter by asking again whether or not God has rejected His people. And once more he responds, "May it never be!"

In Romans 9:1-4 Paul specifically states that the promises that God made to the Jewish people are still valid. Also in Romans 9:27 he reminds his readers that God has determined to save a remnant of the Jews. And he repeats this in Romans 11:26 where he declares that "all Israel will be saved," referring to the remnant that the Bible says will accept Jesus as Messiah at the end of the Tribulation (Zechariah 12:10).

The Source of anti-Semitism

Satan is the source of all anti-Semitism. He hates the Jews with a passion for several reasons:

- He hates them because God provided both the Bible and the Messiah through them.

- He hates them because God called them to be His Chosen People.

- He hates them because God has promised to save a great remnant of them.

- He hates them because God loves them.

The result is that he works overtime to plant seeds of hatred in people's hearts toward the Jews. He is determined to destroy every Jew on planet earth so that God cannot keep His promise to save a great remnant. He tried to annihilate them in the Holocaust. He failed. He will try to destroy them once again during the last half of the Tribulation. He will fail again.

Psalm 129:5-8

5) May all who hate Zion be put to shame and turned backward;

6) let them be like grass upon the housetops, which withers before it grows up;

7) with which the reaper does not fill his hand, or the binder of sheaves his bosom;

8) nor do those who pass by say, "The blessing of the LORD be upon you; we bless you in the name of the LORD." ✤

Questions:

1) The development of Replacement Theology was based on the accusation that because the Jews were the ones who killed Jesus, God washed His hands of them and replaced Israel with the Church. Read Acts 4:27 and list below the ones that the verse says were responsible for the death of Jesus. Is there any person in particular who is missing from the verse?

_____

_____

2) Those who espouse Replacement Theology argue that the Jews lost their title to the land of Canaan either because of their disobedience or because the promise was fulfilled at some time in the past. Read Deuteronomy 12:1, Psalm 89:30-35 and Psalm 105:8-11. Based on these verses, do you think the Jewish people have lost the title to their land?

_____

_____

3) The segment of the New Testament that has been most ignored in the history of Christian teaching and preaching is Romans 9-11. Read these three chapters. Why do you think they have been ignored?

_____

_____

4) The advocates of Replacement Theology argue that the return of the Jewish people to their homeland in the 20th Century and the re-establishment of their state are accidents of history and have no spiritual or biblical relevance. Read Isaiah 11:10-12, Ezekiel 37:1-12 and Zechariah 10:6-12. What do you think?

_____

_____

5) Deuteronomy 7:6-9 says the Jewish people are the "Chosen People" of God. These are the words of Moses. They were confirmed many years later by the prophet Isaiah (Isaiah 41:8-9). What do you think it means to be the "Chosen People" of God? Does it mean they are saved? Read Isaiah 43:10 for a clue to the answer to this question. Finally, do you think they remain today the "Chosen People" of God?

_____

_____

_____

_____

Lesson 11

New Testament Prophecy

> **Fact:** *The New Testament contains both First and Second Coming Prophecies about the Messiah.*

Key Scripture: *"We also have the prophetic message as something completely reliable, and you will do well to pay attention to it, as to a light shining in a dark place . . ."* (2 Peter 1:19 – NIV).

Prophecies about the First Advent of the Messiah are not confined to the Old Testament. This is a truth that is often overlooked.

New Testament Sources

The Gospels contain a number of prophecies about the First Advent. A good number of them are clustered around the birth of Jesus.

Angels spoke prophecies about the Lord's First Coming to Joseph (Matthew 1:20-21) and Mary (Luke 1:26-37), and also to the priest Zacharias (Luke 1:13-17). Prophecies were given to the shepherds of Bethlehem (Luke 2:9-14). There were also several prophecies which the Holy Spirit prompted from people connected with the birth of Jesus — people like the parents of John the Baptist (Zacharias in Luke 1:67-79 and Elizabeth in Luke 1:41-43).

Mary, the mother of Jesus was given a prophetic song (Luke 1:46-55). And two aged prophets named Simeon (Luke 2:25-35) and Anna (Luke 2:36-38) were given prophetic messages when the parents of Jesus took Him to the temple to dedicate Him to God.

John the Baptist, who was a prophet of God, made several prophetic statements about his cousin, Jesus (Matthew 3:11-12). And Caiaphas, the High Priest at the time of Jesus' death, was directed by the Holy Spirit to make a prophetic utterance about the death of Jesus and its significance (John 11:49-52).

Jesus, "The Prophet"

The bulk of the New Testament prophecies concerning events related to the First Advent came from the mouth of Jesus Himself. Fifteen hundred years earlier, Moses had prophesied that the Messiah would be a prophet (Deuteronomy 18:15 & 18). This is the reason that John the Baptist was asked if he was "The Prophet" (John 1:21). He denied that he was (John 1:21-23).

Later, when Jesus began His ministry, His miraculous signs caused the people to cry out, "This is truly the Prophet who is to come into the world" (John 6:14 and John 7:41).

Jesus certainly operated as a prophet. He spoke voluminous prophecies concerning His Second Advent. He also spoke prophetically about events that would occur during His First Advent — or which would result from it.

The Subject Matter

Concerning His First Coming, the topic Jesus gave the most attention to was His death and resurrection. Repeatedly, He told His disciples that He would be killed and that He would rise from the dead on the third day after His death (Matthew 16:21).

Another topic He prophesied about in detail was the Holy Spirit. He stated that He would send the Spirit after His departure, and He prophesied what the work of the Spirit would be (John 14:26).

The Significance

The 100% accuracy of Jesus' prophecies about Himself are proof positive that He was God in the flesh. He was also totally accurate in His prophecies about individuals (Matthew 26:31-34), the Jews (Matthew 23:37-38), the city of Jerusalem (Luke 21:5-6), and the Church (Matthew 16:18-19). There is no doubt that Jesus was "The Prophet" whom Moses told his people to watch for — the One who would also be the Messiah of God.

He made frequent comments about His Second Advent. He stressed the certainty of His return and the fact that He would return in wrath to execute the vengeance of God (Matthew 16:27).

Jesus also emphasized the certainty of judgment and reward for all — both the just and the unjust. He taught there would be degrees of blessing for the righteous and degrees of punishment for the unrighteous. He particularly focused on the rewards waiting for those who accepted Him in faith. He stressed the reward of eternal life, but He also outlined a breathtaking array of other rewards — some that would go to all believers and other, specialized awards, which would be given for distinguished service in the kingdom.

Jesus' most profound prophetic pronouncement was His "Olivet Discourse" delivered to His disciples on the Mount of Olives during the last week of His life. It provides a panoramic survey of the signs we are to look for which will signal the season of His return (Matthew 24).

The Revelation of Jesus

The prophecies of Jesus do not end with the Gospels. Keep in mind that the book of Revelation is a revelation of Jesus to John. The letters to the seven churches of Asia, recorded in Revelation 2 and 3, are letters from Jesus. They contain many prophetic statements, particularly about the glorious rewards that await those who "overcome."

The New Testament ends with a prophetic pronouncement by Jesus. It contains His last recorded words: "Yes, I am coming quickly!" (Revelation 22:20).

The Epistles

Peter, Paul, and John often speak prophetically in the Epistles. Paul spends three full chapters in Romans (9-11) discussing the future salvation of a Jewish Remnant. In Romans 1:18-32 he gives us a detailed glimpse of the perverted nature of end time society. In Romans 8:18-25 he provides an inspiring picture of the future redemption of the universe.

Two of Paul's epistles, 1 and 2 Thessalonians, are almost entirely devoted to prophecy about the return of Christ. In these letters we find the most detailed description of the Rapture that is contained in the Bible (1

Thessalonians 4:13-18). Paul also gives a lot of detailed information about the "day of the Lord" in 1 Thessalonians 5 and 2 Thessalonians 2.

Most of what we know about the glorified bodies of the Redeemed comes from the description which Paul gives in 1 Corinthians 15 and 2 Corinthians 5. In his letters to Timothy, Paul elaborates on the signs that will signal the Lord's return, particularly the signs of society (2 Timothy 3:1-5). Paul also spends considerable time in his writings exhorting his readers to live godly lives as they look for the Second Coming (Romans 13, 1 Timothy 6, and Titus 2).

John's prophetic statements in his epistles relate almost exclusively to the antichrist spirit that will prevail in the end times (1 John 2:18-29). Peter writes much more extensively about the end times in his epistles. In 2 Peter 3 he prophesies the development of the scientific theory of Uniformitarianism, one of the cornerstones of Evolution. In that same passage, he provides a dramatic picture of the reshaping of the heavens and earth by fire.

The writer of Hebrews directs his prophetic comments toward the cosmic struggle for dominion over the earth. He points out that although Jesus won that dominion back from Satan by His work on the Cross, Jesus is not yet exercising that dominion, and will not do so until He returns to reign over the world (Hebrews 2:5-8).

The most ancient Second Coming prophecy in the Bible is contained in the book of Jude, verses 14-15. In these verses Jude quotes a vision attributed to Enoch in the seventh generation from Adam. In the vision Enoch saw the Lord returning to pour out the wrath of God on the ungodly.

The Book of Revelation

The last book in the New Testament focuses on the Tribulation period and the wrath of God that will be poured out on all men to motivate them to repentance. It presents the story of the final crushing of Satan and the glorious triumph of Jesus. It provides a brief look at the Lord's millennial reign and then concludes with an intriguing glimpse of the incredible new Jerusalem that will serve as the eternal home of the Saints on the new earth.

One common myth is the idea that Revelation 20 provides all the information that the Bible contains about the Millennium. The truth is that Revelation 20 reveals very little information about the millennial reign. It tells us that the reign will last 1,000 years, but the Jewish Rabbis had deduced that long before Revelation was written. It says Satan will be bound at the beginning of the Millennium, something that can easily be deduced from Old Testament prophecies about the peace and righteousness that will prevail during that time. It states that the Saints will reign with Jesus, but that had already been specifically prophesied in many Old Testament passages (see, for example, Daniel 7:14,18,27). The revolt of Satan at the end of the Millennium is new information, but not the fact that his ultimate fate will be total defeat (Daniel 11:45).

The vast majority of the information we have about the nature of the Millennium is provided by Old Testament prophecy, particularly the prophecies of Isaiah. The Millennium is not a New Testament concept confined to one chapter in Revelation.

Revelation does provide us with our most detailed information about the Eternal State. Even so, what it reveals merely whets the appetite and stimulates the imagination. The fact of the matter is that the Bible tells us very little about the Eternal State except that the Redeemed will have glorified, immortal bodies and will live in God's presence in a new Jerusalem on a new earth. But what an exciting prospect that is! Romans 8:18 says "that the sufferings of this present time are not worthy to be compared with the glory that is to be revealed to us."

The many glorious promises concerning the future that are contained in New Testament prophecy should provoke us to cry out, "Maranatha!" (1 Corinthians 16:22). ✚

Questions:

1) Read Matthew 24:4-14. How many categories of Second Coming signs can you find in this passage? Name them.

_____

_____

2) Read 1 Thessalonians 4:13-18. What do you think this passage is talking about?

_____

3) Read 2 Timothy 3:1-5. Do you see any of these end time signs in our society today?

_____

_____

4) Read 2 Timothy 4:1-4. Do you see this prophecy being fulfilled in the Church today?

_____

_____

5) Read Romans 1:18-28. Do you think any of these verses apply to our nation today?

_____

_____

6) Read Revelation 2 & 3 and note all the rewards that Jesus promises to give to "overcomers."

_____

_____

Lesson 12

The Church in Prophecy

Fact: *There is both bad news and good news for the Church in Bible prophecy.*

Key Scripture: *". . . upon this rock I will build My church and the gates of Hades will not overpower it"* (Matthew 16:18).

There are both negative and positive prophecies in the Bible concerning the Church in the end times. The negative ones are really awful, but the positive ones are wonderfully glorious.

The Bad News

The picture of the Church-at-large in the end times is not a very pretty one.

Apostasy — For one thing, the Bible prophesies that the Church will be racked by apostasy. Jesus Himself prophesied that "many will fall away" (Matthew 24:10). Likewise, Paul said the Antichrist cannot be revealed until "the great apostasy" takes place (2 Thessalonians 2:3).

Paul reveals the source of the apostasy in 2 Timothy 3:5 — "Men will hold to form of religion but will deny its power." The fulfillment of this prophecy began in the 1920s with the ascendancy of the German School of Higher Criticism. This school of thought, which quickly swept American seminaries, advocated that the Bible should be approached like any other piece of literature — with a critical eye. The concepts of the special inspiration and inerrancy of the Bible were rejected. The Bible came to be viewed as Man's search for God rather than God's revelation to Man. As a human product, it was considered to be full of myth, legend, and superstition.

This assault on the integrity of God's Word opened the floodgates of apostasy. Before long, Christian theologians and ministers were laughing about the virgin birth of Jesus, discounting His miracles, casting doubt on His resurrection and flatly denying His promise to return.

And that is where we are today, caught up in the midst of a gross apostasy which says, "Believe what you want. The important thing is to be sincere. There are many roads to God." All of which makes a liar of Jesus who said: "I am the way, and the truth, and the life; no one comes to the Father but through Me" (John 14:6). The result is that there are a lot of sincere people who are sincerely going to Hell.

Cultism — A second set of prophecies warn that the Church will be assaulted by cultic deception in the end times. Jesus emphasized this point repeatedly in His Olivet Discourse (Matthew 24:5, 11 & 24). And Paul underlined it in the strongest possible language when he wrote: "The Spirit explicitly says that in later times some will fall away from the faith, paying attention to deceitful spirits and doctrines of demons" (1 Timothy 4:1).

The fulfillment of these prophecies began in the 19th Century with the rise of Mormonism and its demonic teaching that Jesus is the brother of Lucifer, one of thousands of Gods created by the super god, Adam, an exalted man. The Jehovah's Witnesses were next on the scene with their perverted teaching that Jesus is the Archangel Michael.

The 20th Century witnessed the rapid multiplication of the cults, just as prophesied. Today, life-long Christians who do not know why they believe what they profess to believe are being sucked into the cults by the tens of thousands.

Heresies — A third group of prophecies indicate that in the end times the Church will be assailed by doctrinal error. These are doctrines that do not damn the soul but which confuse and weaken the spirit.

In 2 Timothy 4:3-4, Paul says: "For the time will come when they will not endure sound doctrine; but wanting to have their ears tickled, they will accumulate for themselves teachers in accordance to their own desires and will turn away their ears from the truth, and will turn aside to myths." There are many popular myths in Christendom today that either rob people of the power of their faith or else deceive them into practicing a presumptuous faith.

Worldliness — A fourth characteristic prophesied about the Church in the end times is that it will be compromised and corrupted by worldliness. The prophetic picture of this worldly church is found in Revelation 3:14-22, where the church at Laodicea is described.

The seven churches depicted in Revelation 2 and 3 are symbolic of seven periods of church history. The church at Laodicea, the last to be presented, is representative of the type of church that will prevail in Christendom at the end of the Church Age.

The picture is a pathetic one. The Church is apathetic, neither hot nor cold. The apathy is a product of the Church's adoption of a worldly attitude expressed in the words, "I am rich, and have become wealthy, and have need of nothing." Jesus responds with a scathing rebuke: "You do not know that you are wretched and miserable and poor and blind and naked" (Revelation 3:17).

The Bible makes it clear that the Church will become so compromised in the end times that it will get in bed with the world, resulting in the disintegration of society to the point that it will become as immoral and violent as in the days of Noah (2 Timothy 3:1-5 and Matthew 24:37).

The Good News

Is there any good news about the Church in end time prophecy? Yes, there is.

Outpouring of the Spirit — The incredibly good news is that the Bible prophesies a great pouring out of God's Spirit in the end times to empower those who are receptive to stand against the onslaught of Satan.

The prophecy is found in Joel 2:28-30. The context before the passage (verse 23) makes it clear that there will be two outpourings of the Spirit (the "early and latter rain"). The early rain occurred at Pentecost when the apostles were anointed with the Spirit. The final outpouring will begin after the Jews are regathered to their land and re-established as a nation (verses 18-27).

We have been in the period of the "latter rain" ever since the re-establishment of the state of Israel on May 14, 1948. The Spirit is being poured out, and the gifts of the spirit are being manifest in a way unparalleled since the First Century.

There are many other manifestations of the outpouring of God's Spirit on the Church today. In 1949 the ministry of Billy Graham took off like a rocket when William Randolph Hearst featured the evangelist in his myriad of publications. Through Graham's utilization of modern technology, he was able to reach the entire world with the Gospel.

The same has been true of the Jesus Film which was produced by Campus Crusade in 1979. It has since been translated into more than 1,600 languages and has been shown to over seven billion people, resulting in over 530 million decisions for Christ.

Modern technology has also made it possible to produce translations of the Bible quicker than ever before. The result is that the Bible is now readily available in all the major languages of the world.

This explosion in outreach has produced an exponential increase in conversions. In 1800 the conversion rate was 100 per day. By 1900 it had increased to 1,000 per day. Today the rate is an astronomical 175,000 per day! And 3,500 new churches are opening every week worldwide.

Among faithful Christians, this great anointing of the Spirit is pro-ducing a remnant that is immersed in the Word, committed to righteousness, crucified to self, dedicated to prayer, surrendered in worship, zealous for evangelism and yearning for the soon return of Jesus. It is this remnant that will stand firmly for Jesus until the day He returns for His Church.

The Rapture — Bible prophecy gives the Church the wonderful promise that it will be removed from the world before God pours out His wrath in the Tribulation (1 Thessalonians 4:13-18). See the chapter 14 for details.

The Second Coming — The Church is promised that it will return with Jesus at the time of His Second Coming (Revelation 19:7-8,14). This means the Church Age saints will witness His victory at Armageddon and His coronation as King of kings and Lord of lords. See lesson 18 for details.

The Millennium – The Church is promised that it will reign with Jesus when He returns to earth to reign for a thousand years from Jerusalem (Daniel 7:13-14,18,27, 2 Timothy 2:12 and Revelation 20:4). See lesson 19 for details.

The Eternal State — The Church is promised that it will reside forever on a new, perfected earth in the presence of God the Father and Jesus (Revelation 21:1-7). See lesson 20 for details.

Paul summed up the future blessings of the Church when he wrote:

> For I consider that the sufferings of this present time are not worthy to be compared with the glory that is to be revealed to us (Romans 8:18). ✤

Questions:

1) How do you explain the existence of end times prophecies about the Church that portray the Church as being energized by the Spirit for greater outreach while also experiencing increasing apostasy? Read Matthew 13:24-30,36-43.

_____

_____

_____

2) Read 2 Timothy 4:1-3. What apostate or heretical doctrines in the Church today come to your mind when you read this passage?

_____

_____

_____

3) Read Revelation 3:14-17. Do you think these verses describe the condition of the Church in America today?

_____

_____

4) Three times in Matthew 24 (verses 5,11,24) Jesus prophesied that in the end times there would be an explosion of false christs and their cultic groups. How would you define a cult? What are some of their common characteristics?

_____

_____

_____

5) The first prophecy in the Bible to specifically mention the Church was given by Jesus in Matthew 18. He said He would build it upon "this rock." What rock?

_____

_____

6) Many people today believe that church membership is unimportant. Others think they can fulfill church membership by watching a church service on TV. What do you think, and why? Read Hebrews 10:25.

_____

_____

Lesson 13

A Chronology of End Time Events

> **Fact:** *Bible prophecy gives us certain definite events to look for in the future.*

Key Scripture: *"No eye has seen, no ear has heard, and no mind has imagined what God has prepared for those who love him. But it was to us that God revealed these things by His Spirit. For His Spirit searches out everything and shows us God's deep secrets"* (1 Corinthians. 2:9-10, NLT).

The Bible reveals some spectacular events that will happen in the future — not everything, but enough to give us a living and vibrant hope.

Compiling a Chronology

Constructing a chronology of future end time events is not an easy chore. That's because such a chronology is nowhere given in detail in the Scriptures. Instead, it must be pieced together bit by bit, like a jigsaw puzzle, drawing from passages in both the Old and New Testaments.

No one prophet is given the entire end time scenario. And keep in mind that when looking into the future, prophets see only mountain tops that God wants them to see, and not the valleys in between. (See the illustration on page 22.)

A good example can be found in 2 Peter 3:10-13. This passage portrays the return of the Lord as if it will be the time when the heavens and earth will be consumed with fire.

Now, if this was the only passage in the Bible about the Lord's return, we could conclude that the heavens and earth will be burned up when the Second Coming occurs.

But there are many other passages in both the Old and New Testaments that make it clear that the Lord will reign here on earth for a thousand years after His return, and then the heavens and earth will be renovated with fire.

As is the case with all biblical doctrines, all passages related to any doctrine must be considered, and not just isolated ones.

Because assembling an end time chronology is like solving a puzzle, it is not possible to chisel a particular chronology in stone. There is room for disagreement. This is not an area for dogmatism.

The chronology that follows is based on a literal or plain sense interpretation of what the Bible says about the end times. The exact timing of some of the events — like the War of Gog and Magog and the Rapture — is not revealed in the Scriptures.

So, what is presented on the next two pages is based in some cases on inferences rather than outright declarations.

A Proposed Chronology

The War of Psalm 83 — This is a war of annihilation against Israel that is launched by an inner circle of nations that have a common border with Israel. We know from passages like Zechariah 12:6-9 that Israel will win this war.

The War of God and Magog — Ezekiel 38 and 39 picture another war against Israel by an outer circle of nations led by Russia. All the nations named as allies of Russia are Muslim states today. God will intervene and supernaturally destroy the attacking armies. Some place this war at the beginning of the Tribulation. Others put it three and a half years before the Tribulation.

The Rapture — This is the appearing of the Lord in the heavens for His Church, an event that could occur any moment — before, between or after the wars named above. There are no signs for this event and no prophecies that must be fulfilled before it happens. The only thing that appears certain about its timing is that it will occur before the Tribulation begins (1 Thessalonians 1:10).

A Gap — It appears there will be a gap of time between the Rapture and the beginning of the Tribulation during which time a panicked world will respond to a dynamic leader in Europe (the Antichrist) who will seem to have all the answers.

Emergence of the Antichrist — The Bible says the Antichrist will come from the people who destroyed the Temple in 70A.D. — the Romans (Daniel 9:26). Most likely he will emerge from the European Union since the Bible indicates that the Roman Empire will be revived in the end times (Daniel 2:36-45).

A Covenant — The Antichrist will make a covenant with Israel (Daniel 9:27) that will mark the beginning of the Tribulation. The exact nature of this covenant is not revealed, but it is usually assumed that it will constitute a guarantee of Israel's security and will enable the Jews to rebuild their Temple.

The Tribulation — The Antichrist will launch a military campaign to take over the world. During the first half of the Tribulation (3½ years), his conventional war (Revelation 6) will morph into a nuclear one (Revelation 8 & 9).

Desecration of the Temple — By the middle of the Tribulation the Antichrist will have conquered the whole world (Revelation 13:7). At that point, he will go to Jerusalem, enter the rebuilt Temple, and declare himself to be god.

The Revolt of the Jews — The Jewish people will reject the Antichrist as their Messiah, and he will respond by attempting to annihilate them (Revelation 12:13-17). The Jews will flee into the area that is known today as Jordan.

The Second Coming — At the end of the seven years of the Tribulation, Jesus will return in glory to the Mount of Olives in Jerusalem (Zechariah 14:1-9). He will speak a supernatural word that will instantly destroy the Antichrist and his armies (Zechariah 14:12-15).

Salvation of the Jews — When Jesus appears in the heavens, the remaining remnant of the Jews will repent (Zechariah 12:10) and receive their Messiah (Matthew 23:37-39).

Resurrection — The New Testament saints were resurrected at the time of the Rapture. At the Second Coming, all Old Testament saints, as well as Tribulation martyrs, will be resurrected and glorified.

Judgment — Jesus will judge all Jews and Gentiles who are left alive at the end of the Tribulation (Matthew 25:31-46 and Ezekiel 20:33-38). Those who have accepted Him as Lord and Savior will be allowed to enter the Millennium in the flesh. Those who have not done so will be consigned to death and Hades.

Binding of Satan — Satan will be bound in the bottomless pit where he can no longer deceive the nations (Revelation 20:1-3).

Reign — Jesus and His glorified saints will reign for a thousand years over those in the flesh (Revelation 20:4-5). The earth will be flooded with peace, righteousness and justice as the waters cover the seas (Isaiah 2:1-4 and 11:4-9).

Revolt — At the end of the millennium, Satan will be released, and he will rally many of those in the flesh to rebel against the reign of Jesus. The rebels will be destroyed by God, and Satan will be thrown into Hell (Revelation 20:7-10).

White Throne Judgment — All those throughout history who died outside a faith relationship with God will be resurrected and judged of their works to determine their eternal destiny (Revelation 20:11-15). Since no one can be justified by works, all of these people will be consigned to Hell.

Renovation — The heavens and earth will be renovated by fire, burning away the pollution of Satan's last revolt. Out of this fiery inferno will come new heavens and a new, perfect and eternal earth (2 Peter 3:12-13).

Heaven — Heaven will come to earth. The redeemed will live eternally in the presence of God in the New Jerusalem located on the New Earth (Revelation 21:2-7).

Therefore, comfort one another with these words — (1 Thessalonians 4:18). ✤

Quotations:

"In some cases, the actual chronology of a prophetic event is based more on theological inferences than on explicit biblical statements. In view of this, there is room for some disagreement among Christians regarding the timing of some prophetic events." — Ron Rhodes, *The End Times in Chronological Order* (Harvest House, 2012).

"Many religions and worldviews believe history is an endless cycle of events continually repeating themselves, and thus they conclude that life is meaningless because, from their perspective, it is going nowhere. By contrast, the biblical view of history is linear and not circular. That is, history has a beginning and an ending. It is going somewhere and has purpose and meaning. It began in a garden and is moving toward a city, with a cross in between." — Ed Hindson and Tommy Ice, *Charting the Bible Chronologically* (Harvest House, 2016).

Questions:

1) Did you discover anything new to you in the order of end times events presented in this lesson?

_____

_____

2) Why do you think God did not provide a list of end time events in their exact order?

_____

_____

3) What changes would you make in the proposed order of events in this lesson, and why?

_____

_____

4) Amillennialists believe we are living in the Millennium now since the Holy Spirit is in the world. Many also believe we are simultaneously in the Tribulation since the Church is suffering persecution. Do you think this lines up with what the Bible says?

_____

_____

_____

5) One aspect of chronology that is confusing to many people is the fact that the book of Revelation contains "flash-forwards." We are accustomed to flash-backs in literature, but not flash-forwards. The reason the book contains flash-forwards is because God knows the future. And thus, at certain points in the book of Revelation, readers are presented with a flash-forward to assure them that Jesus is going to triumph in the end. For examples of flash-forwards, read: Revelation 6:12-17, 11:15-18 and 14:1-5,14-20. There is a rhythm to the book's narration. Each time the description of a series of horrible events is completed, the reader is catapulted forward to the Second Coming to assure the reader that Jesus is going to triumph. Thus. Revelation 14:14-20 is like a movie preview of what is to come. Do you see this in your reading of these passages?

_____

_____

_____

Lesson 14

The Rapture

> **Fact:** *The Church is promised deliverance from this world before the Tribulation begins.*

Key Scripture: *"Because you have kept the word of My perseverance, I also will keep you from the hour of testing, that hour which is about to come upon the whole world, to test those who dwell on the earth"* (Revelation 3:10).

The Rapture is a glorious event which God has promised to the Church. The promise is that someday very soon, at the blowing of a trumpet and the shout of an archangel, Jesus will appear in the sky and take up His Church, living and dead, to Heaven.

The Word

The term, Rapture, comes from a Latin word, *rapio*, that means to catch up, to snatch away, or to take out. It is, in turn, a translation of the Greek word, *harpadzo*.

Rapture is a Biblical word that comes right out of the Latin Vulgate translation of the Bible. The word is found in 1 Thessalonians 4:17. In the New American Standard Version, the English phrase, "caught up," is used. The same phrase is used in the King James and New International Versions.

A Promise to the Church

The concept of the Rapture was not revealed to the Old Testament prophets because it is a promise to the New Testament Church and not to the saints of God who lived before the establishment of the Church. Jesus will return as a bridegroom for His bride, and that bride consists only of Church Age saints.

The saints of Old Testament times will be resurrected at the end of the Tribulation and not at the time of the Rapture of the Church. Daniel reveals this fact in Daniel 12:1-2 where he says that the saints of that age will be resurrected at the end of the "time of distress."

Biblical References

The first clear mention of the Rapture in Scripture is found in the words of Jesus recorded in John 14:1-4. Jesus said, "I will come again, and receive you to Myself; that where I am, there you may be also."

The most detailed revelation of the actual events related to the Rapture is given by Paul in 1 Thessalonians 4:13-18. He says that when Jesus appears, the dead in Christ (Church Age saints) will be resurrected and caught up first. Then, those of us who are alive in Christ will follow "to meet the Lord in the air."

Paul mentions the Rapture again in 1 Corinthians 15 — his famous chapter on the resurrection of the dead: "Behold, I tell you a mystery;

we shall not all sleep, but we shall be changed, in a moment, in the twinkling of an eye, at the last trumpet" (verses 51 and 52).

Paul's reference here to being changed is an allusion to the fact that the saints will receive glorified bodies that will be imperishable, immortal and perfected (1 Corinthians 15:42-44, 50-55 and Isaiah 35:5-6).

A Summary

To summarize, these passages teach that the shout of an archangel and the blowing of a trumpet will herald the sudden appearance of Jesus in the heavens (1 Thessalonians 4: 16). The dead in Christ will be resurrected and rise up to meet the Lord in the sky. Then, those saints who are alive will be "caught up" to the Lord. Paul concludes his description in 1 Thessalonians 4:18 by encouraging his readers to "comfort one another with these words."

And truly the Rapture is a comforting thought! Consider the promises contained in the concept of the Rapture. Jesus will bring with Him the spirits of those who have died in Him (1 Thessalonians 4:14). He will resurrect their bodies in a great miracle of re-creation; He will reunite their bodies with their spirits; and He will then glorify their bodies, making them immortal. And those believers who are living will not even taste death. Rather, they will be caught up to the Lord, and in transit, they will be translated from mortal to immortal.

A Return in Two Stages

There are two detailed descriptions of the Lord's return in the New Testament, one written by the Apostle Paul and the other by the Apostle John (see the diagram on page 66).

The passage in 1 Thessalonians 4 presents a scene of love, mercy, and grace. The picture that is painted by Revelation 19 is one of vengeance and wrath. In the Thessalonian passage, the Lord appears in the sky, but does not descend to the earth. In the Revelation account, He comes to the earth. Zechariah 14 says He will return to the Mount of Olives from which He ascended into Heaven.

One of the most significant differences between the two passages relates to the Church. In the Thessalonian account, the Lord comes for the purpose of taking His Church, both the dead and living members, out of this world. In Revelation, by stark contrast, He returns *with* His Church. This is indicated in Revelation 19:14 where it says that "the armies which are in heaven, clothed in fine linen, white and clean were following Him on white horses." We know these people constitute the Church, because the same group is described a few verses before (verses 7 and 8) as being the "bride" of Christ.

Thus, in Paul's description of the Lord's return, He is portrayed as coming *for* His Church, to deliver believers from the "wrath that is to come" (1 Thessalonians 1:10). But in John's description, Jesus is portrayed as returning *with* His Church in great wrath. In Thessalonians, Jesus returns as a Deliverer. In Revelation, He comes back as a Warrior. In one scene He is coming to claim the righteous; in the other, He returns to condemn the unrighteous.

A Problem in Reconciliation

What is going on here? How could these two passages be talking about the same event? How can they be reconciled?

There is really only one way to reconcile them and that is to conclude that *they are describing two separate events.* That, in turn, implies rather clearly that there are going to be *two* future comings of the Lord.

One of those — the one described in 1 Thessalonians 4 — will be more of an appearing than a coming, for the Lord will not actually return to the earth. He will, instead, appear in the heavens and supernaturally draw the Church, living and dead, to Him.

The Post-Tribulation Rapture

Amillennials and some Premillennials have tried to deal with these two conflicting descriptions of the Lord's return by combining them at the end of the Tribulation into one event. Their concept is that the Lord will appear in the heavens, the Church will be caught up to Him, and then He and the Church will immediately return to earth.

There are some serious problems with this concept which has been described as a "Yo-Yo Rapture." The first problem is that it destroys the imminence of the Lord's return. Over and over in the New Testament we are told that the Lord's return is imminent and that we should therefore always be ready for His return (Matthew 24:36,42,44,50 and 25:13).

Imminence means it could occur at any moment. But that is impossible if you combine the Rapture with the Second Coming because there are too many prophecies that must be fulfilled before the Second Coming can occur. For an event to be imminent, it must be capable of occurring at any moment.

A second major problem with the Post-Tribulation concept of the Rapture is that it eliminates a population to enter the Millennium in the flesh. Just think about it — if the Rapture and the Second Coming occur together at the end of the Tribulation, then all believers are glorified at that point and all unbelievers are consigned to death and to Hades. Where are the people in the flesh that will occupy the earth during the Lord's reign?

A third problem with the Post-Trib Rapture is that it makes no sense in view of the many New Testament admonitions that we are to live looking for the return of Jesus. Paul, for example, told Titus we are to live "looking for the blessed hope and the appearing of the glory of our great God and Savior, Christ Jesus" (Titus 2:13). If we are not going to see Jesus until the end of the Tribulation, then we should be living looking for the Antichrist and not Jesus Christ.

The Pre-Tribulation Rapture

It is only when you place the Rapture before the Tribulation that you end up with a population for the Millennium. That population will consist of all those, both Jew and Gentile, who accept Jesus during the Tribulation and live to the end of that terrible period.

A Pre-Tribulation Rapture solves another problem as well. The Bible teaches that believers are immune to the wrath of God. And since the seven years of the Tribulation constitute the pouring out of God's wrath from beginning to end, the Church must be taken out of the world before that period begins. And that is exactly what the Scriptures teach. Go back to the beginning of this lesson and read the opening verse taken from the book of Revelation. Then, consider 1 Thessalonians 1:10 which says that we are "to wait for His Son from heaven, whom He raised from the dead, that is Jesus, who rescues us from the wrath to come."

Jesus Himself said that when we see the end times signs "begin to take place," we are to "keep alert at all times, praying in order that you may have strength to escape all the things [the events of the Tribulation] that are about to take place . . ." (Luke 21:35).

An Objection

One of the major objections to the Pre-Trib Rapture concept is that "it is too new to be true." This objection is based on the belief that the concept did not come into being until the early 19th Century. But recent research has revealed that the concept existed in a variety of denominations in England dating back as far as the 17th Century.

The important point to keep in mind is that the date of doctrine is really irrelevant. The only thing that matters is whether or not it lines up with what the Bible says. In the 16th Century, when Martin Luther revived the true Gospel of salvation by grace through faith, his critics dismissed his new idea as "too new to be true," despite the fact that it was clearly one of the fundamental truths of the New Testament.

Further, it should be kept in mind that both Jeremiah and Daniel were told that many end time prophecies would not be understood until the time came for them to be fulfilled (Jeremiah 23:20, Jeremiah 30:24 and Daniel 12:8-9).

Hope or Terror?

To summarize, we should be looking for two future comings of the Lord — one at the beginning of the Tribulation, the other at the end. The first, the Rapture, will be the appearing of the Lord for His Church. The second, the Second Coming, will be the return of the Lord to the earth to "judge and wage war" against the enemies of God (Rev. 19:11). ✤

A Comparison of the Rapture with the Second Coming

The Rapture 1 Thessalonians 4	The Second Coming Revelation 19
Jesus **appears** in the heavens	Jesus **returns** to earth
Jesus appears **for** His Church	Jesus returns **with** His Church
Jesus appears as a Deliverer	Jesus returns as a Warrior
Jesus appears in Grace	Jesus returns in Wrath
Jesus appears as a Bridegroom	Jesus returns as a King

Questions:

1) Read 2 Peter 2:4-9. Do you see a Pre-Tribulation Rapture inferred in this passage?

_____

_____

2) The first three chapters of Revelation focus on the Church. After John is raptured to Heaven in chapter 4, the Church is not mentioned again until Revelation 23:16. Doesn't this lack of mention of the Church during the description of the Tribulation in chapters 6-19 indicate a Pre-Tribulation Rapture? Could John's rapture in chapter 4 be symbolic type of the rapture of the Church?

_____

_____

3) If the Church is to go through the horrors of the Tribulation before the Rapture occurs, could the last verse of Paul's description of the Rapture (1 Thessalonians 4:18) really be applicable?

_____

_____

4) If the Church is destined to go through the Tribulation, then shouldn't Christians live looking for the Antichrist rather than Jesus Christ?

_____

5) There are some people who try to put the Rapture in the middle of the Tribulation. To do so, they have to argue that the Seal Judgments are not judgments of God but are judgments of Man and Satan. Read Revelation 6. Do you think this chapter teaches that the Seal Judgments are from God?

_____

_____

6) Make a list of all the prophetic events that must take place before the Second Coming of Jesus. Now, if the Rapture is one and the same as the Second Coming, then where is the imminence of the Lord's return?

1) _____   6) _____

2) _____   7) _____

3) _____   8) _____

4) _____   9) _____

5) _____   10) _____

Lesson 15

The Tribulation

> **Fact:** *The Church Age will be followed by a seven year period of unparalleled tribulation during which time God will pour out His wrath on this world.*

Key Scripture: *". . . for then there will be a great tribulation, such as has not occurred since the beginning of the world until now, nor ever shall"* (Jesus speaking in Matthew 24:21).

The Bible gives us a lot of information about the Tribulation. The entire book of Zephaniah is devoted to it, in addition to many other Old Testament passages, like Isaiah 24. Fourteen chapters in the book of Revelation focus on it (Revelation 6-19).

But despite all this information, there are many myths concerning the Tribulation that circulate among Christians. For example, many argue that the first half of this time period will be peaceful and that only the second half will be characterized by intense warfare. Other misconceptions relate to the Antichrist and the Church.

The Biblical Basis

Before we consider some of these myths and misconceptions, let's familiarize ourselves with the concept of the Tribulation. Where does the idea come from, and what does it mean?

The first mention of the Tribulation in the Bible is found in Deuteronomy 4:27-30. Before the Children of Israel entered the Promised Land, Moses warned them that if they were unfaithful to God, they would be scattered among the nations. He then prophesied that "in the latter days" they would come under "distress," and the result would be their "return to the Lord."

Centuries later, Jeremiah used the same terminology when he referred to the Tribulation. He called it "the time of Jacob's distress" (Jeremiah 30:7). In like manner, Daniel called it "a time of distress," and he prophesied it would be the worst period of trouble in the history of the Jewish people (Daniel 12:1). Malachi stated it would be a time of refining for the Jews, as when silver is purified by fire (Malachi 3:1-4). And Zechariah used the same imagery when he prophesied that two-thirds of the Jewish people will perish during this time. Of the remnant remaining, he wrote, "I [the Lord] will bring the third part through the fire [and] refine them as silver is refined . . ." (Zechariah 13:8-9).

The Scope

The Jews will not be the only ones to suffer during this period of unparalleled trouble. The Bible makes it clear that all the nations of the world will experience catastrophic calamities.

Isaiah says it will be "a day of reckoning" for all the nations of the world (Isaiah 2:10-17). Zephaniah says that "all the earth will be devoured in the fire of God's jealousy" (Zephaniah 1:18). Here's how the psalmist Asaph put it: "A cup is in the hand of the Lord, and the wine foams . . . surely, all the wicked of the earth must drain and drink down its dregs" (Psalm 75:8).

The Length

The prophet Daniel defined the length of the Tribulation. He said God would accomplish all His purposes for the Jewish people during a period of 70 weeks of years (490 years). Sixty-nine of those weeks of years (483 years) would lead up to the death of the Messiah. The final week of years would occur at the end of the age, right before the return of the Messiah (Daniel 9:24-27). This concluding week of years (7 years) corresponds to the Tribulation for, as Daniel put it, it will mark the time when "the prince who is to come" will "make desolate" — a reference to the Antichrist.

The timing established by Daniel is confirmed in the book of Revelation where the Tribulation is divided into two periods of 3½ years each (Revelation 11:3,7 and 13:5). The dividing point between the two halves of the Tribulation will occur when the Antichrist reveals himself by entering the rebuilt Temple in Jerusalem, stopping the sacrifices, and declaring himself to be god (Matthew 24:15, 2 Thessalonians 2:3-4, and Revelation 13:5-6).

The Starting Point

When will this terrible period begin? The Bible says in general terms that it will start after the Jews have been regathered and have been reestablished in their homeland and in their sacred city of Jerusalem.

Specifically, the Bible says it will begin at a time when all the world comes together against Israel over the issue of who will control the city of Jerusalem (Zechariah 12:2-3). In short, we are on the very threshold of the Tribulation today as we witness the United Nations, the European Union, the Vatican, and the Arab nations demanding that the Jews surrender their sovereignty over Jerusalem.

The specific event that will mark the seven year count down of the Tribulation will be the signing of a covenant between Israel and the Antichrist that will most likely guarantee Israel's safety and allow the Jews to rebuild their Temple (Daniel 9:27).

The Nature

The unparalleled horror of the Tribulation is spelled out in detail in both the Hebrew Scriptures and the New Testament. Isaiah wrote that it will be a day of "the terror of the Lord" when "the pride of men will be abased" (Isaiah 2:10,17,19). Zephaniah proclaimed that it will be a "day of wrath," "a day of trouble and distress," and "a day of destruction and desolation" (Zephaniah 1:15). Men will stumble around like they are blind and "their blood will be poured out like dust" (Zephaniah 1:17).

This dreary picture is echoed in the New Testament. Jesus said it will be a time of tribulation "such as has not occurred since the beginning of the world until now, nor ever shall" (Matthew 24:21). In fact, Jesus said it will be so terrible that if it were not stopped at the end of seven years, it would result in the destruction of all life (Matthew 24:22). The Apostle John states that the chaos will be so great that the leaders of the world will crawl into caves and cry out for the rocks of the mountains to fall upon them (Revelation 6:15-16).

Misconceptions

With this biblical background, let's turn our attention now to some of the misconceptions that exist regarding the Tribulation. Five of the major ones are listed below:

1) The Antichrist will rise to world power through cunning, flattery, and deception. It is true that he will rise to power in Europe, using skilled diplomacy (Daniel 8:23,25), but he will gain world power through war (Daniel 8:24).

2) The whole world will flock to the Antichrist in awe and adoration. Not a chance! The Muslim world will reject him. And Africa, Asia and Latin America will not willingly agree to be placed under European colonialism once again.

3) The Jews will accept the Antichrist as their Messiah. Never! They will accept him as a political savior, but when he declares himself to be god in the middle of the Tribulation, they will reject him.

4) There will be 3½ years of peace followed by 3½ years of war. Not according to the book of Revelation. It pictures human carnage from the beginning to the end of the Tribulation.

5) The Antichrist will be the most brilliant and effective leader in world history. For a while it will seem that way, but in the middle of the Tribulation, he will become obsessed with destroying the Jewish people and that obsession will lead to his downfall.

6) The Church will go through the Tribulation. This view is based primarily on the fact that the book of Revelation mentions persecution of "saints" during the Tribulation, even war against them (Revelation 13:7). But these passages refer to those who will become Christians during the Tribulation.

The Purpose

What's it all about? Why is there going to be such carnage? How could a God of grace, mercy and love allow such an outbreak of unbridled terror and bloodshed?

One reason is to satisfy the justice of God. Yes, God is characterized by grace, mercy and love, but He is also a God of perfect justice, righteousness and holiness. Therefore, He must deal with sin. His justice demands it. Even His love compels it. How could a God of true love simply overlook the actions of a murderer or a pedophile?

A second reason for the Tribulation is to bring people to salvation. Amazingly, even when God pours out His wrath, His fundamental purpose is not to destroy but to save. Isaiah 26:9 explains it this way: "When the earth experiences Your judgments, the inhabitants of the world learn righteousness." Most hearts will be hardened, but some will be brought to repentance.

Man is frivolous about sin. God is serious. The Tribulation will be a graphic expression of how serious God is about Mankind's rebellion against Him. ✤

Overview of Tribulation Events

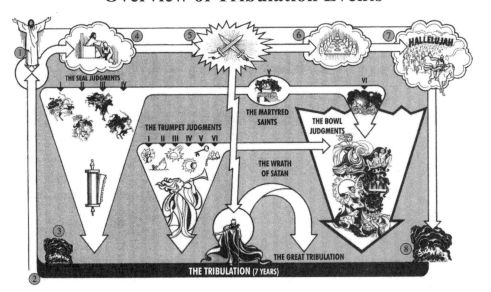

(**Note:** The numbers below correspond to the numbers on the diagram above.)

1) Jesus appears in the heavens (1 Thessalonians 4:16).

2) The Church is Raptured to meet Jesus in the sky (1 Thessalonians 4:17).

3) The Antichrist launches a war to conquer the world. It begins as a conventional war (The Seal Judgments) and morphs into a nuclear war (The Trumpet Judgments). See Revelation chapters 6, 8 and 9.

4) The judgment of Church Age Saints occurs in Heaven. They are judged of their works to determine their degrees of rewards (2 Corinthians 5:10).

5) In the middle of the Tribulation, Satan will try to take God's throne once more, resulting in a war in the heavens between the forces of Satan and the angelic army led by the Archangel Michael (Revelation 12:7-12). Satan is defeated and thrown to earth where he possesses the Antichrist (2 Thessalonians 2:3; Revelation 13:3-5). The Antichrist launches a campaign of annihilation against both the Jews and those who have accepted Jesus during the Tribulation.

6) The Church, the Bride of Christ, celebrates its union with its Bridegroom, Jesus, in Heaven while God pours out His final judgments on earth in the form of the Bowl Judgments (Revelation 16:1-17 and 19:7-8).

7) The Church Age Saints return to earth with Jesus to participate in His thousand year reign over all the earth (Revelation 19:11-16).

8) Jesus destroys the Antichrist and his armies at Armageddon (Revelation 19:17-21 and Zechariah 14:1-15).

Notice that the book of Revelation contains "flash-forwards." Two of them are illustrated in the diagram above. The first is found in Revelation 6:12-17 where the opening of the last seal propels the reader forward to the Second Coming. The second is found in Revelation 11:15-18 where the seventh trumpet also takes the reader to the Second Coming.

Questions:

1) The table of contents of the book of Revelation is found in Revelation 1:19. It divides the book into three parts: "the things you have seen," "the things which are," and "the things that will take place after these things." What chapters would you assign to each section?

_____

_____

2) The book of Revelation refers to "saints" throughout the Tribulation. These are people who accept Jesus as Lord and Savior during the Tribulation. With the Church gone, due to the Rapture, how will these people come to a saving knowledge of Jesus? How will they hear the Gospel?

_____

_____

3) Take a look at Revelation 5:9-10. This is a song being sung in Heaven before the throne of God. Do you believe it clearly teaches that there will be a reign of Jesus on the earth?

_____

_____

4) Chapter 12 of Revelation contains a lot of symbols. How would you identify the "woman clothed in the sun" (verse 1) and the "male child" (verses 5)?

_____

_____

5) Chapter 17 of Revelation reveals a woman with the words "Mystery Babylon" written on her head. Read chapters 17 and 18. How would you identify this "Mystery Babylon"?

_____

_____

6) Jesus states in the book of Revelation that He is "coming quickly" (Revelation 22:12 & 20). It's been 2,000 years since He spoke these words. So, what did He mean by "quickly"?

_____

_____

Lesson 16

The Antichrist

> **Fact:** *The Bible teaches that a person called the Antichrist will take over every nation in the world during the Tribulation.*

Key Scripture: *"It was also given to him [the Antichrist] to make war with the saints and to overcome them, and authority over every tribe and people and tongue and nation was given to him"* (Revelation 13:7).

The Bible teaches that in the end times, right before the return of Jesus, the greatest political leader in the history of Mankind will emerge from Europe. After taking over that area by diplomatic cunning and deceit, he will launch a military campaign that will result in his acquiring "authority over every tribe and people and tongue and nation" (Revelation 13:7).

His Kingdom

His empire will be the most extensive in all of history, encompassing the entire world, and his rule will be the most demonic the world has ever experienced.

He will begin his rise to power as a dynamic, charismatic, insightful, visionary leader who will astound the world with the cleverness of his solutions to world problems. He will appear to be the savior of the world. But as he consolidates his power, his true nature will be revealed.

He will emerge as a Satan possessed and empowered person who hates God and is determined to annihilate both Christianity and Judaism. For this reason, he is identified in scripture as the Antichrist (1 John 2:18), for he will stand against God and His anointed one, Jesus Christ.

His Origin

Where will this sinister person come from? Some have speculated that he will come out of Syria since one of his prophetic types in history — Antiochus Epiphanes (215-164 B.C.) — was a Syrian tyrant. But Antiochus was actually of Greek heritage. Could he therefore be a Greek? It is not likely.

It is much more likely that he will rise out of the heartland of the old Roman Empire and that he will be of Italian descent. This conclusion is based upon a statement in Daniel 9:26. In that passage the Antichrist is referred to as "the prince who is to come," and he is identified as being from the people who "will destroy the city and the sanctuary."

We know from history that both Jerusalem and the Jewish Temple were destroyed by the Romans in 70 A.D. Therefore, according to Daniel, the Antichrist must be of Roman heritage.

Will he be a Jew? Many assume he will be because Jesus said, "I have come in My Father's name, and you do not receive Me; if another shall come in his own name, you will receive him" (John 5:43). Based on this statement, people ask, "How could the Jews possibly receive a Gentile as their Messiah?"

But the Bible does not teach that the Jews will receive the Antichrist as their Messiah. It teaches they will accept him as a great political leader and diplomat and that they will put their trust in him as the guarantor of peace in the Middle East.

But the moment he reveals himself as the Antichrist by desecrating the Jew's rebuilt Temple and blaspheming God, the Jewish people will revolt. They will reject him as Messiah, and he will respond in fury by attempting to annihilate them.

The Antichrist does not have to be a Jew. And, in fact, the Bible makes it clear that he will be a Gentile. In Revelation 13:1 he is portrayed as a "beast coming up out of the sea." The sea is used consistently throughout the prophetic scriptures as a symbol of the Gentile nations (Daniel 7:3, Isaiah 17:12 and Isaiah 60:5).

His Character

The Bible is very specific about the character of the Antichrist, and the picture it paints is a disgusting one. The most detailed information can be found in the book of Daniel.

Over and over emphasis is given to the Antichrist's mouth. He will boast non-stop about himself (Daniel 7:8). He will "speak monstrous things against the God of gods" (Daniel 11:36). He will be "given a mouth speaking arrogant words and blasphemies" (Revelation 13:5). First and foremost, he is going to be a braggart and a blasphemer. (See the chart on page 76.)

He will be strong willed and reckless in his determination to have his way. He will show contempt for human traditions and will, of course, change even the calendar so that it will no longer be related to the birth of Jesus (Daniel 7:25).

Another point that is emphasized repeatedly is that the Antichrist will be possessed by Satan, just as Judas was (Luke 22:3). Daniel says his power will be mighty, "but not by his own power" (Daniel 8:24). Paul says his coming will be "in accord with the activity of Satan, with all power and signs and false wonders" (2 Thessalonians 2:9). John says that Satan will give his power and authority to the Antichrist (Revelation 13:2).

Because he will be demonized, he will be a man who cannot be trusted. Psalm 52:2 says he will be a "worker of deceit." Psalm 55:21 says his speech will be "smoother than butter" but his heart will be filled with war. Psalm 5:6 calls him "a man of bloodshed and deceit." In Psalm 43:1 he is referred to as a "deceitful and unjust man."

Daniel indicates that he will be a sexual pervert, most likely a homosexual. As Daniel puts it, the Antichrist will show no regard "for the desire of women" (Daniel 11:37).

The overall picture is that of an ego-maniac who abhors God and exploits people for his own purposes. He is deceptive and ruthless. He is a man devoid of integrity. This is probably the reason that when Jesus returns, John characterizes Him as the "Faithful and True" One (Revelation 19:11), in contrast to the Antichrist who has been both unfaithful and untrue.

His Career

The Rapture itself is likely to be the event that will catapult the Antichrist to power. This is because the Rapture will produce international chaos and panic. The Antichrist, energized by Satan (Daniel 8:24), will seem to have all the answers to the world's problems. He will take over the European Union through skillful intrigue (Daniel 8:23) and will establish his headquarters in Rome (Revelation 17:3,9,18).

The seven year time period of the Tribulation will actually begin when the Antichrist negotiates a treaty that will bring true peace to the Middle East, enabling the Jews to rebuild their Temple (Daniel 9:27). With his European base consolidated and peace achieved in the Middle East, he will set forth to subdue the whole world.

The world will resist him, and the result will be a Third World War in which he "will destroy to an extraordinary degree" (Daniel 8:24). This war will initially result in the death of one-fourth of humanity (Revelation 6:8). As the Tribulation approaches its mid-point, this war will escalate into a nuclear holocaust that will result in the deaths of an additional one-third of those still alive (Revelation 8 and 9).

It will be an empty victory because in the process of his conquest, one-third of the earth will be destroyed and half its population will be killed. He will then consolidate his "victory" by instituting a one-world economy and a one-world religion.

The key to his economic control will be a mark that each person will have to bear on their right hand or on their forehead (Revelation 13:16-18). No one will be able to buy or sell unless they have this mark. The mark will consist of "either the name of the beast or the number of his name" (Revelation 13:18).

His religious control will be exercised by a false prophet who will head up his pagan religious system (Revelation 13:11-15). He will force all of humanity to worship the Antichrist. He will be a deceiver who will astound people with "great signs" that appear miraculous in nature.

In order to consolidate this Satanic religious system, the Antichrist will launch a great persecution of all those who have placed their faith in the true God since the Rapture of the Church (Revelation 12:13-17). The result will be a mass slaughter of believers (Revelation 7:9-14).

His Fate

The Bible indicates that as the Antichrist becomes obsessed with the Jews, he loses interest in his worldwide empire, and segments of that empire begin to revolt. The core of the revolt is centered in the Asian nations who raise an army of 200 million and send it marching across Asia toward Israel where they hope to engage the Antichrist in a decisive battle for their freedom.

Daniel says that while the Antichrist and his armies are rampaging around the Middle East, looting the nations and killing the Jews, the Antichrist suddenly hears "rumors" that "disturb him" (Daniel 11:40-44). He evidently hears about the great Asian army coming to challenge him. He responds by consolidating his forces "between the seas and the beautiful Holy Mountain" (Daniel 11:45). This is the same area that is referred to in Revelation as the Valley of Armageddon (Revelation 16:16).

We are told that the Euphrates River dries up at this time and the great Asian army crosses to engage the Antichrist and his armies in battle (Revelation 16:12). As they fight, the Lord Jesus Christ breaks from the heavens, returns to the Mount of Olives in Jerusalem, and speaks a supernatural word that causes all the armies to drop dead in their tracks. "Their eyes rot in their sockets and their tongues rot in their mouths" (Zechariah 14:12), and the valley is filled with blood up to the horses' bridles for a distance of two hundred miles (Revelation 14:20).

Paul says the Antichrist will be slain by "the breath of the Lord" (2 Thessalonians 2:8). John confirms this imagery, saying the Lord will make war against the Antichrist "with the sword of His mouth" (Revelation 2:16). Daniel adds that the Antichrist's "dominion will be taken away, annihilated and destroyed forever" (Daniel 17:26). Daniel also says that the Antichrist will be thrown into "the burning fire" (Daniel 7:11).

John confirms the fate of the Antichrist in Revelation when he says that both the Antichrist and the False Prophet will be thrown into "the lake of fire which burns with brimstone" (Revelation 19:20) where "they will be tormented day and night forever and ever" (Revelation 20:10). This means that the Antichrist and the False Prophet will be the first occupants of Hell. (Satan will not be confined there until the end of the Millennium — Revelation 20:10). ✢

Characteristics of the Antichrist

Description	Little Horn Daniel 7	Small Horn Daniel 8	Willful King Daniel 11	Man of Lawlessness 2 Thess. 2
Braggart / Egotist	✔	✔	✔	✔
Blasphemer of God	✔	✔	✔	✔
Contemptuous	✔	✔	✔	✔
Persecutor of Believers	✔	✔		
Insolent		✔		
Deceptive / Shrewd		✔		
Demonic		✔		✔
Destructive		✔		✔
Willful		✔	✔	
Sexually Perverted			✔	
Militarist			✔	
Materialist			✔	

Questions:

1) Do you believe the Antichrist could be alive today? And, if so, why?

_____

_____

2) Read Revelation 13:1-3. Do you think these verses indicate that the Antichrist will be killed and resurrected from the dead?

_____

_____

3) The Apostle John states in 1 John 2:18-22 that there were antichrists in his day and implies this will be the case throughout history. What do you think this means?

_____

_____

4) Some have started claiming in recent years that the Antichrist will be a Muslim. Do you think this is a possibility? Explain your answer.

_____

_____

_____

5) Read Daniel 7:8-11. What impresses you the most about this description of the Antichrist and why?

_____

_____

6) In Revelation 11:7 and 17:8, the Antichrist is described as a "beast" from the "abyss." Could this indicate that he will be a demon in human form?

_____

_____

7) The Antichrist will be a part of a Satanic trinity on earth during the Tribulation. Who will be the other two members of this trinity? Read Revelation 12:3,9-12 and 13:11-18.

_____

_____

Lesson 17

The Wars of the End Times

Fact: *The Bible reveals that there will be a total of nine wars in the end times.*

Key Scripture: *"It was also given to him [the Antichrist] to make war with the saints and to overcome them, and authority over every tribe and people and tongue and nation was given to him"* (Revelation 13:7).

The only end times war that most people have ever heard of is the War of Armageddon which, as will be explained later, is not going to be a true war at all. So, people are very surprised when they discover that Bible prophecy reveals nine end times wars. Let's take a brief look at each one.

(1) The War of Extermination
Psalm 83

The psalm states that the immediate neighbors of Israel will launch a war for the purpose of "wiping out Israel as a nation" (verse 4). The nations described as being a part of this nefarious effort are those with a common border with Israel today (verses 6-8). The rest of the psalm is a prayer for the victory of Israel (verses 9-18).

The outcome of the war is not stated, but we know from other scriptures that Israel will be victorious. For example, in Zechariah 12:6 we are told that in the end times Israel will be like "a firepot among pieces of wood and a flaming torch among sheaves, so they will consume on the right hand and on the left all the surrounding peoples . . ."

(2) The First War
of Gog & Magog
Ezekiel 38 & 39

But the security provided by the Psalm 83 war will not last long. The Arab nations will turn to their natural ally, Russia, and cry out for help.

And the Russians will be very happy to respond, for they have always dreamed of taking the oil fields of the Middle East. They will, therefore, launch an invasion for the stated purpose of helping the Muslims destroy Israel, but their unstated agenda will be to use the Arab invitation as an excuse to expand their sovereignty over all the Middle East. This ulterior motive is described in Ezekiel 38:12 where it says the Russians will come "to capture spoil and to seize plunder."

The invading armies will be supernaturally destroyed by God "on the mountains of Israel" (Ezekiel 39:4). The Lord will accomplish this destruction through earthquakes, pestilence, hail storms, fire, brimstone, and battlefield confusion (Ezekiel 38: 19-22).

The greatest mystery concerning this war is its timing. Most have placed it at the beginning of the Tribulation, but increasingly in recent years, the tendency has been to place it before the beginning of the Tribulation. One of the most important reasons for this conclusion is that Ezekiel 39:9 says the Jews will spend seven years burning the weapons captured in the war. But the book of Revelation says they will flee the land 3½ years into the Tribulation in order to escape the Antichrist.

(3) The Conventional War of the Tribulation – Revelation 6

This is the war the Antichrist will launch to conquer the world. It is likely to focus on the Muslim nations that are certain to reject his rule. But many other nations in the world will also have to be subdued. One-fourth of humanity will die in this war which is pictured in Revelation as the Seal Judgments.

(4) The Nuclear War of the Tribulation – Revelation 8 & 9

The Antichrist's conventional war will morph into a nuclear holocaust, resulting in the deaths of another one-third of Mankind. A hint that this war will be a nuclear one is to be found in Revelation 16:2 & 11 where we are told that "loathsome and malignant sores" will afflict people at the end of the Tribulation, something that would be a natural consequence of radiation poisoning.

It could very well be that this nuclear war is what Jesus had in mind when He stated that in the end times men will faint from fear over the expectation of the things coming upon the world, "for the powers of the heavens will be shaken" (Luke 21:26).

This war is portrayed in the book of Revelation in chapters 8 & 9 as a series of "Trumpet Judgments."

(5) The War in the Heavens Revelation 12

The next end time war is totally different in nature from all the rest. It is a supernatural one that will occur in the heavens in the middle of the Tribulation. It is most likely prompted by an attempt of Satan to once again take the throne of God.

Satan and his angels are opposed in this war by Michael and his angels. Michael is an archangel who is pictured in the Hebrew Scriptures as the commander-in-chief of the armies of God (Daniel 10:13,21 and 12:1). Michael and his angels prevail in this war, and Satan is cast down to earth. His access to God's throne is cut off (Revelation 12:9-10).

When this happens, Satan realizes that his time is short because he knows Bible prophecy (Revelation 12:12). In his rage, Satan decides to destroy the Jewish people, and this decision leads to the next war.

(6) The War Against the Jews and the Saints – Revelation 12

When Satan is cast down to earth, he will possess the Antichrist (Revelation 13:2) and inspire him to annihilate all the Jews. This is the reason that Jesus referred to the last half of the Tribulation as "the great tribulation" (Matthew 24: 21) — not because this half will be worse than the first half, but because the wrath of Satan will be focused on the Jews.

Some of the Jews of Israel will flee to a place in the "wilderness" where they will be supernaturally protected by God (Revelation 12:13-14). Many believe this hiding place will be the ancient city of Petra, located inside a box canyon in modern Jordan. There is good reason for this assumption because Daniel 11:41 says the Antichrist will be prevented from conquering Jordan.

But despite this supernatural protection of a remnant in Jordan, Zechariah 13:8 indicates that two-thirds of the Jewish people worldwide will be killed by the Antichrist during this time, and Revelation 12:17 says the Antichrist will also war against the "offspring" of Israel — namely, those "who keep the commandments of God and hold to the testimony of Jesus." This is a reference to all those who accept Jesus as their Lord and Savior during the Tribulation, both Jews and Gentiles.

(7) The Middle East Campaign of the Antichrist – Daniel 11

Daniel 11:40-45 describes a military campaign of the Antichrist in the Middle East that occurs at the end of the Tribulation.

These verses and related verses in Revelation could very well indicate that when the Antichrist becomes insanely obsessed with destroying the Jews and the Saints, the nations of the world will see an opportunity to rebel against him. The Antichrist responds by invading "the Beautiful Land" and subduing all the area except Jordan.

Just as the Antichrist seems to be completely victorious, he hears "rumors from the East and from the North" that deeply disturb him. He retreats with his armies to the area "between the seas" where "he will come to his end." The geographical description here of a location between the Mediterranean Sea and the Sea of Galilee corresponds to the Valley of Armageddon.

The rumors that frighten him are, in part, the news that "the kings from the East" (Revelation 16:12), who are bringing huge armies from Asia, have arrived at the Euphrates River and are ready to cross into Israel to challenge him. The rumors from the North could relate to a reconstituted rebellious army from Russia.

(8) The War of Armageddon Joel 3, Zechariah 14 and Revelation 19

It appears that just as the armies from the East and the North start arriving in the Valley of Armageddon to challenge the Antichrist, the Lord breaks from the heavens, returns to the Mount of Olives, speaks a supernatural word, and all the armies are instantly destroyed (Zechariah 14).

In other words, there really is no such thing as the "Battle of Armageddon." The armies are assembled to do battle, but the Lord annihilates all of them in a microsecond "with the breath of His mouth" (2 Thessalonians 2:8).

Joel 3:16 says the Lord will "roar from Zion" and "utter His voice from Jerusalem." Isaiah 10:16 says the result will be "a wasting disease." Zechariah 14:12 says it will be a plague that will cause the flesh of the soldiers "to rot while they stand on their feet." Their eyes will melt in their sockets and their tongues will dissolve in their mouths. It will be like the explosion of a neutron bomb.

(9) The Second War of Gog & Magog Revelation 20

Mercifully and joyfully, the "battle" of Armageddon will be followed by one thousand years of peace, as the reign of Jesus from Jerusalem results in the world being filled with righteousness and justice (Isaiah 11:

4-5,9). But to produce this result, Jesus will have to rule with a "rod of iron" (Psalm 2:9 & Revelation 19: 15).

Thus, when Satan is released at the end of the Lord's millennial reign (Revelation 20:7), the majority of those in the flesh will unite in one last rebellion against God that is pictured in Revelation 20:7-9. Led once again by Gog & Magog, this war is often confused with the war of Ezekiel 38 and 39. But the two are very different. The Ezekiel war pictures Russia coming against the nation of Israel with certain specified allies. In Revelation 20 Russia is portrayed as leading all the nations of the world against Jesus Christ.

The rebellious nations will be destroyed by God with fire from heaven (Revelation 20:9).

The Abolition of War

The Second War of Gog & Magog will be the final war of history. Following it, God will take the Redeemed off this earth and place them in the New Jerusalem on the new earth.

This new world will inaugurate eternal peace. War will be gone forever. The hope of Mankind will not be achieved by diplomats. It will be a gift of God through Jesus Christ who died to redeem Mankind and all the cosmos. ✤

The Unparalleled Carnage of the Tribulation

The death toll of the Tribulation is beyond imagination. There are seven billion people on planet earth today. Assuming that one billion of those will be taken in the Rapture of the Church, a total of six billion would enter the Tribulation.

The conventional war of the Antichrist (the Seal Judgments) will result in the deaths of one-fourth of humanity, equaling 1.5 billion people. Of the remaining 4.5 billion, one-third of them will die in the nuclear war of the Antichrist (The Trumpet Judgments). That will amount to another 1.5 billion. So, by the middle of the Tribulation, one-half of all those who entered the Tribulation will be dead (a total of 3 billion!).

Additionally, during the second half of the Tribulation, two-thirds of the Jews will be killed. There are 14 million Jews in the world today, so the number of Jews that will die in this second holocaust will be about 9.5 million, a number greater than died in the Nazi holocaust.

Quotation:

"Whether we are wrestling with individual insecurity or national insecurity, the Bible comforts us that God is in control not only of our individual lives — including the timing and circumstances of our deaths — but also of human history. And through biblical prophecy, God has given us a portrait of what things will look like on this planet during the last days. If biblical prophecy teaches us anything, it is that God is in complete control of human history and its culmination." — Ron Rhodes.

Questions:

1) The first atomic bomb was detonated on July 16, 1945 in New Mexico. The only such bombs to be used in warfare were dropped on Japan in August of 1945. In the years since that time, no nuclear weapons have been used in warfare. Do you think this is due to God's restraining hand? Could the unleashing of nuclear weapons during the Tribulation be an example of what is called "God's wrath of abandonment"? This is the kind of wrath that occurs when God lifts His restraining hand and allows Mankind's evil to multiply.

_____

_____

_____

2) Do you think the use of nuclear weapons is inevitable? If so, why?

_____

_____

3) Read Revelation 8 & 9. Would you agree that these chapters are describing a nuclear war?

_____

_____

4) Do you think it is possible that the Antichrist's wars to take over the world could be used as God's vengeance to annihilate the religion of Islam?

_____

_____

5) Read Isaiah 10:16, Isaiah 11:4, Zechariah 14:12 and Revelation 19:15. Based on these verses, would you agree that there really will not be such a thing as the "Battle of Armageddon"?

_____

_____

6) Why would the Lord's millennial reign of perfect peace, righteousness and justice provoke people to join Satan in a revolt against Jesus in the Second War of Gog & Magog?

_____

_____

Lesson 18

The Second Coming

> **Fact:** *The Second Coming will end the Tribulation and inaugurate the Millennium.*

Key Scripture: *"I will gather all the nations against Jerusalem . . . Then the Lord will go forth and fight against those nations . . . And in that day His feet will stand on the Mount of Olives . . . And the LORD will be king over all the earth . . ."* (Zechariah 14:2-4,9).

The two great prophetic symbols of the Messiah in the Old Testament are the Suffering Lamb (Isaiah 53:7) and the Conquering Lion (Isaiah 31: 4-5). He is pictured with the same symbols in New Testament prophecy (Revelation 5:5-6). The Suffering Lamb prophecies were fulfilled in the First Coming of Jesus. The Conquering Lion prophecies will be fulfilled when Jesus returns to pour out the wrath of God on those who have rejected the love, grace and mercy God has offered through His Son.

Because the Old Testament prophecies picture the Messiah with two such starkly different images, the rabbis concluded there would be two Messiahs — Messiah Ben-Joseph (the lamb) and Messiah Ben-David (the lion). They did not understand that there would be only one Messiah who would fulfill both roles.

The Certainty
of the Lord's Return

We can be assured that there will be a Second Coming because the Bible prophesies it and Jesus Himself promised it.

Ironically, what is probably the oldest Second Coming prophecy in the Bible is found in the New Testament and not the Old. It is in the book of Jude, where in verses 14 and 15 we are told about an ancient prophetic vision: ". . . Enoch, in the seventh generation from Adam, prophesied, saying, 'Behold, the Lord came with many thousands of His holy ones, to execute judgment upon all, and to convict all the ungodly of all their ungodly deeds . . .'"

Another ancient prophetic statement about the Messiah's Second Coming can be found in the book of Job, which many scholars believe is the oldest book in the Bible. It is contained in words spoken by Job when he said (Job 19:25-27):

> As for me, I know that my
>   Redeemer lives,
> And at the last, He will take
>   His stand on the earth.
> Even after my skin is de-
>   stroyed,
> Yet from my flesh I will see
>   God;
> Whom I myself shall behold . . .

In this passage Job is saying by inspiration of the Holy Spirit that a day will come when he will be resurrected from the dead, and that will be when his Redeemer stands on the earth. We know from Daniel 12:1-2 that the resurrection of Old Testament Saints will not take place until the end of the Tribulation, so when Job speaks of the Messiah standing on the earth, he must be speaking of the Second Coming.

Many of the Psalms, all the Major Prophets and almost all the Minor Prophets look forward to the day when the Messiah will come to earth to live in Jerusalem and reign over all the world. In the New Testament, Peter, Paul and John all affirm that the Messiah will return to reign.

The Archangel Gabriel promised Mary that her son would be given the throne of David and "will reign over the house of Jacob forever" (Luke 1:32-33). This did not happen at the Lord's First Coming, so it must be referring to His Second Coming.

After His resurrection, when Jesus ascended into Heaven, two angels appeared to His disciples and told them that He would one day return in just the same way — bodily and visibly (Acts 1:10-11).

Most important, Jesus Himself promised that one day He would return (Revelation 22:12). People usually think of Jesus' last words on this earth as being the ones He spoke on the Cross. But 65 years after His death, burial and resurrection, Jesus appeared to the Apostle John on the Isle of Patmos, and the very last words He spoke were "I am coming soon" (Revelation 22:20).

The Timing

These words of Jesus raise a very important issue: How could Jesus mean He was returning "soon" when it has now been 2.000 years since His ascension?

The Apostle Peter answered this question when he wrote that to God, "a thousand years is like a day" (2 Peter 3:8). He then explained the reason for the delay: "The Lord is not slow about His promise, as some count slowness, but is patient toward you, not wishing for any to perish, but for all to come to repentance" (2 Peter 3:9).

Further, Jesus' comment was meant to give us a sense of imminence — the realization that He could return at any moment. A sense of imminence is important because it inspires holy living and evangelism.

This raises another issue that relates to the timing of the Second Coming. How can the Second Coming be imminent if there are so many prophecies that have to be fulfilled before it can happen — events like the rebuilding of the Temple, the revelation of the Antichrist and the Tribulation? The answer is that the Lord's return to this earth is not imminent. Rather, it is the appearing of the Lord in the Rapture that is imminent.

Remember from lesson 14 that the Second Coming consists of two stages — first, the Lord's appearing in the Rapture and then, second, the Lord's return to earth.

The Rapture is imminent and can occur at any moment. The Second Coming is not imminent. The Bible reveals its precise timing: it will occur 2,520 days after the Antichrist signs a covenant with Israel (Revelation 11:3 and 12:6). So, the Lord's actual return to the earth will occur at the end of the Tribulation.

Resurrections

At the Second Coming, there will be a resurrection of Old Testament Saints (Daniel 12:2) and Tribulation Martyrs (Revelation 20:4).

The Bible speaks of two resurrections in the end times. Jesus refers to them as the "resurrection of life" and the "resurrection of judgment" (John 5:29). The Apostle Paul confirmed this when he said that according to the prophets, there will be "a resurrection of both the righteous and the wicked" (Acts 24:15).

Based on these two references one could easily conclude there are going to be two resurrections at the time of the Second Coming — one for the just and the other for the unjust. But when you dig further into the Scriptures, you find more than two resurrections. That's because when the Bible speaks of two resurrections, it is talking about two in kind and not two in number.

We know this for certain because the resurrection of the righteous occurs in stages. Paul refers to these stages in 1 Corinthians 15:20-23 where he explains that there is an order to the resurrection of the righteous: "Christ the first fruits, after that those who are Christ's at His coming." Actually, as pictured in the diagram on page 87, the resurrection of the righteous occurs in three stages: 1) Christ "the first fruits," 2) The Church Age Saints at the Rapture, and 3) Tribulation Martyrs and Old Testament Saints at the Second Coming. The "second resurrection" of the unjust will occur all at once at the end of the Millennium when all those throughout history who died outside a faith relationship with God are raised and judged.

Judgments

Resurrection will be followed by judgment. The apostle Paul emphasized the certainty of judgment. In Romans 2:16 he wrote, "God will judge the secrets of men through Christ Jesus." And in Romans 14:10, 12 he stated, "We shall all stand before the judgment seat of God . . . So then each one of us shall give account of himself to God." The writer to the Hebrews summed it up succinctly: "It is appointed for men to die once and after this comes judgment" (Hebrews 9:27).

When and where will the judgment of the redeemed take place? The Bible indicates the judgment of believers who have lived and died during the Church Age will occur in Heaven before the judgment seat of Jesus, immediately following the Rapture of the Church (2 Corinthians 5:10 and Revelation 19:6-9).

Those who are saved and martyred during the Tribulation will be judged at the end of that period when they are resurrected at the Second Coming of Christ (Revelation 20:4). Old Testament saints will also be resurrected at this time and judged (Daniel 12:1-2).

All who live to the end of the Tribulation — both Jews and Gentiles — will also be judged at the Second Coming of Jesus. The Gentile judgment is portrayed in Matthew 25:31-46 as "the sheep and goat judgment." The judgment of living Jews is portrayed in Ezekiel 20:33-38. Those who have received Jesus as their Lord and Savior will be allowed to enter the Millennium in the flesh. Those who have not will be consigned to death and Hades (Matthew 25:46).

All the unrighteous who have ever lived will be resurrected and judged at the end of the millennial reign of Jesus. This terrible judgment is pictured in Revelation 20:11-15. It is called the "Great White Throne Judgment."

We are told that the wicked also will be judged of their works. But their judgment will be radically different from the judgment of the Redeemed. Whereas the Redeemed are judged of their works to determine their degrees of reward, the lost are judged of their works to determine their eternal destiny. And since no one can be justified before God by their works (Ephesians 2:8-10), all will be condemned to Hell.

The unjust are also judged for another reason. There are going to be degrees of punishment (Luke 12:35-48; 20:45-47). There is a popular myth in Christendom that says, "All sin is equal in the eyes of God." That is not true. The only way in which all sin is equal is that any sin, whether a white lie or murder, condemns us before God and necessitates a Savior.

But all sin is not equal in the eyes of God. For example, Proverbs 6:16-19 lists seven sins that the Lord particularly hates, including "hands that shed innocent blood." And the Bible makes it very clear that idolatry is a sin that is especially heinous in the eyes of God (Exodus 20:3-5).

Because God considers some sins worse than others, there will be degrees of punishment (Revelation 22:12), and these degrees will be specified at the Great White Throne Judgment.

The Interregnum

In politics, an interregnum is the period of time between two successive governments. The Bible reveals that there will be such a period of time between the rebellious rule of the Antichrist and the righteous reign of Jesus Christ.

The interregnum can be found in Daniel 12:11-12. Verse 11 reveals that there will be a 30-day period of time following the last 3½ years of the Tribulation. Verse 12 makes it clear that there will then be an additional 45 days, making a total of 75 days. We are not told exactly what will happen during these days, but it could very well be that the 30-day interval would be used for the various judgments and the additional 45 days for the setting up of the Lord's government and the inauguration of the Millennium. ✦

Quotations:

"The Second Coming of Christ will be so revolutionary that it will change every aspect of life on this planet. Christ will reign in righteousness. Disease will be arrested. Death will be modified. War will be abolished. Nature will be changed. Man will live as it was originally intended he should live." — Billy Graham (1918-2018).

"The first time Christ came to slay sin in men. The second time He will come to slay men in sin." — Arthur W. Pink (1886-1952), a British Bible teacher and author.

An Overview of End Time Resurrections

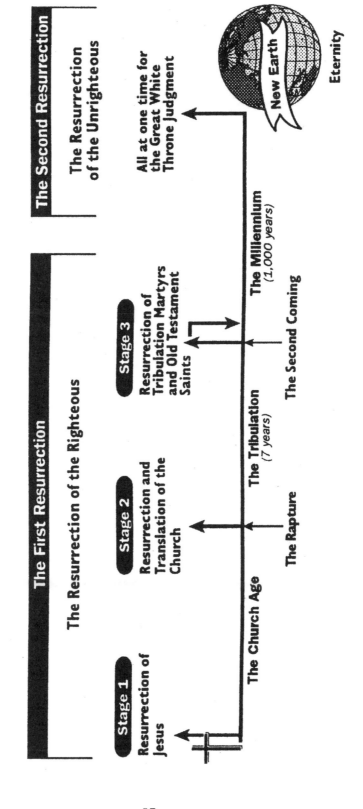

The First Resurrection

The Resurrection of the Righteous

The Second Resurrection

The Resurrection of the Unrighteous

Stage 1
Resurrection of Jesus

Stage 2
Resurrection and Translation of the Church

Stage 3
Resurrection of Tribulation Martyrs and Old Testament Saints

All at one time for the Great White Throne Judgment

New Earth

Eternity

The Church Age

The Rapture

The Tribulation (7 years)

The Second Coming

The Millennium (1,000 years)

Questions:

1) What was the most surprising thing that you learned in this lesson?

_____

2) When the Angel Gabriel appeared to Mary to inform her that she would be the mother of the Messiah, he gave her eight prophetic promises. How many of these have been fulfilled? Are there any yet to be fulfilled at the Second Coming?

(1) You will conceive a child.

(2) You will bear a son.

(3) You shall name Him Jesus.

(4) He will be great.

(5) He will be called the Son of the Most High.

(6) He will be given the throne of David.

(7) He will reign over the house of Jacob.

(8) His kingdom will have no end.

_____

3) Both believers and unbelievers are going to be judged of their works, but for different reasons. Can you explain?

_____

_____

4) The Bible teaches that believers will never be judged of their sins. Can you explain why? Read Isaiah 43:25, 2 Corinthians 5:21 and Hebrews 9:28.

_____

_____

_____

Resurrection vs. Resuscitation

People often ask, "How can Jesus be referred to as the 'first fruits of the resurrection' when the Bible records the resurrections of numerous people before Him?"

The answer is that none of these people, like Lazarus, were resurrected. They were, instead, resuscitated. In other words, they were re-animated to die again at a later time. True resurrection in the biblical sense is resurrection to eternal life.

Lesson 19

The Millennium

Fact: *The Bible teaches that Jesus will return to this earth to reign for a thousand years from Mount Zion in Jerusalem.*

Key Scripture: *"And the LORD will be king over all the earth. On that day there will be one LORD — His name alone will be worshiped"* (Zechariah 14:9 – NLT).

The Bible — both the Old Testament and the New — clearly teaches that Jesus is returning to this earth to reign for a thousand years. The only way to get around that fact is to spiritualize what the Bible says. But keep in mind that the First Coming prophecies meant what they said, and there is no legitimate reason to conclude that the Second Coming prophecies do not mean what they say.

The future reign of Jesus over all the world is called the Millennium, which is Latin for one thousand years. It is mentioned many places in the Old Testament. Two in particular can be found in Isaiah 2:1-4 and Micah 4:1-7. In the New Testament, Revelation 20:1-10 is devoted to it, providing the new information of its duration. This passage says six times that it will last one thousand years.

The Nature of the Millennium

The reign will be worldwide (Isaiah 2:2 and 9:6-7). It will be peaceful in nature (Isaiah 2:4), and the world will be blessed with righteousness (Isaiah 11:4-5) and justice (Isaiah 42:3-4).

The Lord's throne will be established in Jerusalem, for He will occupy the throne of David (Isaiah 2:3). His government will be a theocratic one in which He will serve as king, legislator and judge (Isaiah 33:17-22). The Redeemed will reign with the Lord as princes (Isaiah 32:1). And because the Lord will be reigning from Jerusalem, the nation of Israel will be the prime nation in the world (Isaiah 2:2-3, 49:22-23, and 60:1-62:7).

Isaiah spends a large amount of time outlining the spiritual blessings of the Millennium, the greatest of which is the fact that the glory and holiness of the Lord will be manifested (Isaiah 40:3-5, 52:13-15, 61:3 and 66:18). Holiness will abound (Isaiah 4:2-4), and an attitude of joy and praise will prevail: "And the ransomed of the Lord will return, and come with joyful shouting to Zion, with everlasting joy upon their heads. They will find gladness and joy, and sorrow and sighing will flee away" (Isaiah 35:10).

A rebuilt Temple in Jerusalem will serve as the worship center of the world (Isaiah 2:2-3, 56:6-8, and 60:7b,13). Incredibly, the Shekinah glory of God will hover over the city of Jerusalem like a canopy (Isaiah 4:5). And "the earth will be full of the knowledge of the Lord, as the waters cover the sea" (Isaiah 11:9).

One aspect of the Millennium that is heavily emphasized by the Hebrew prophets is the redemption of nature. The land of Israel will no longer be a place of desolation (Isaiah 62:3-5). Instead, "the fruit of the earth" will be the pride of Israel (Isaiah 4:2). "Waters will break forth in the wilderness," and the deserts will become pools of water (Isaiah 35:6b-7).

In addition to agricultural abundance, the animal kingdom will be restored to its original perfection. Poisonous animals will cease to be poisonous, and meat-eating animals will become herbivorous. All members of the animal kingdom will live together in perfect peace with each other and with Mankind (Isaiah 11:6-9 and 65:25).

In a thrilling passage in Isaiah 65, the prophet reveals that lifespans for those in the flesh will be greatly expanded to "the lifetime of a tree" (Isaiah 65:22). Accordingly, anyone who dies at the age of 100 will be considered a youth (Isaiah 65:20).

Every person will have his own home and vineyard. There will be no homeless or hungry people (Isaiah 65:21-22). All labor will be redeemed (Isaiah 65:23) in the sense that it will be productive, and it will not be confiscated by others.

Disease will be curtailed (Isaiah 33:24), and persons born with physical handicaps will be healed: "Then the eyes of the blind will be opened, and the ears of the deaf will be unstopped. Then the lame will leap like a deer, and the tongue of the dumb will shout with joy" (Isaiah 35:5-6).

These are the descriptions of the literal realities of a literal kingdom, and it is a serious matter to spiritualize them into non-literal meaninglessness. Keep in mind that when Jesus was about to ascend into Heaven, His disciples asked, "Lord, is it at this time You are restoring the kingdom to Israel?" (Acts 1:6). Jesus did not rebuke them for believing there would be a future kingdom. Rather, He simply told them that it was not meant for them to know the timing when the kingdom would be established (Acts 2:7).

The Purpose of the Millennium

The central question concerning the Millennium is "Why?" Why not simply take all believers to Heaven at the Second Coming and be done with this sin-sick world? The reason is that God has made a number of promises that must be fulfilled during the Millennium.

Promises to the Jews — The first reason there must be a Millennium is that God has made promises to the Jews which He will fulfill during that time.

God has promised that He will gather to the land of Israel the remnant of Jews who accept Jesus as their Messiah at the end of the Tribulation (Ezekiel 36:22-28 and Zechariah 10:6-9). He will pour out His Spirit upon this remnant (Isaiah 32:15 and 44:3), greatly expand their numbers and their land (Ezekiel 36:10-11 and 48:1-29), and make them the prime nation in all the world (Isaiah 60-62).

Zechariah says the blessings of God upon the Jewish remnant will be so great in those days that "ten men from all the nations will grasp the garment of a Jew saying, 'Let us go with you, for we have heard that God is with you'" (Zechariah 8:23).

Promises to the Church — A second reason for the Millennium relates to a promise which God has made to the Church. God has promised that the Redeemed in Christ will reign over all the nations of the world.

This promise was given through the prophet Daniel in the following words: "Then the sovereignty, the dominion, and the greatness of all the kingdoms under the whole heaven will be given to the people of the saints of the Highest One; His kingdom will be an everlasting kingdom, and all the dominions will serve and obey Him" (Daniel 7:27).

In the New Testament, Paul repeated the same promise in the simplest of terms: "If we endure, we shall also reign with Him" (2 Timothy 2:12). Jesus affirmed the promise in His letter to the church at Thyatira when He wrote: "And he who overcomes, and he who keeps My deeds until the end, to him I will give authority over the nations; and he shall rule them with a rod of iron . . ." (Revelation 2:26-27).

When John was taken to Heaven for a visit to the throne room of God, he heard a heavenly host singing a song that contained the following verse: "And You have made them [the Redeemed] to be a kingdom and priests to our God; and they will reign upon the earth" (Revelation 5:10).

This promise to the Church of worldwide dominion is going to be fulfilled during the Millennium. That is what Jesus was referring to in the Sermon on the Mount when He said, "Blessed are the gentle, for they shall inherit the earth" (Matthew 5:5).

Jesus will reign as king of the world from Mt. Zion in Jerusalem (Isaiah 24:23 and Zechariah 14:9). The Redeemed, in their glorified bodies, will help Him with His reign by serving worldwide as administrators, judges and spiritual tutors to those who enter the kingdom in the flesh — and to their children (Daniel 7:18,27, Jeremiah 3:15 and Luke 19:11-17).

Promises to the Nations — God has promised that a time will come when the nations will be provided with their greatest dream — namely, worldwide peace.

God has promised to give Mankind and the earth a rest from its wars. But that peace will not come until the Prince of Peace returns. Only then will the nations "hammer their swords into plowshares, and their spears into pruning hooks" (Isaiah 2:4). Only then will we realize the dream of a world where "nation will not lift up sword against nation, and never again will they learn war" (Isaiah 2:4).

Promises to the Creation — God has also made promises to His creation which He will fulfill during the Millennium. God has promised to remove the curse which He placed upon the creation due to the sin of Man. He has promised to deliver the Creation from its bondage to decay and to restore it to its original beauty, balance, and peace (Romans 8:18-23).

The land of Israel will be so radically transformed that visitors will proclaim in amazement: "This desolate land has become like the garden of Eden" (Ezekiel 36:35).

Promises to Jesus — The most important reason for the Millennium is that God is going to use it to fulfill promises which He has made to His

Son. God has promised Jesus that He will be glorified in history (Isaiah 24:23, Isaiah 66:18-19 and 2 Thessalonians 1:7-10).

God also has promised that He will give Jesus dominion over all the world and that He will reign over the nations from Mt. Zion in Jerusalem (Isaiah 2:2-4 and Zechariah 14:1-9).

Psalm 2 presents Jesus in a pre-incarnate appearance speaking to David of His Father's promise: "I will surely tell of the decree of the LORD: He said to Me, 'You are My Son, today I have begotten You. Ask of Me, and I will surely give the nations as Your inheritance, and the very ends of the earth as Your possession. You shall break them with a rod of iron . . .'" (Psalm 2:7-9).

It must be kept in mind that Jesus is currently a "king-in-waiting." Like King David, who had to wait many years after he was anointed before he became King of Israel, Jesus has been anointed King of kings and Lord of lords, but He has not yet begun to rule.

He is currently serving as our High Priest before the throne of God (Hebrews 8:1). He is waiting for His Father's command to return and claim all the kingdoms of this world (Hebrews 2:5-9 and Revelation 19:11-16).

A Final Reason

There is one other purpose for the Millennium that should be noted. God is going to use the Millennium to prove to Mankind once and for all that Satan's religion of Humanism is totally bankrupt.

All Humanists, regardless of their political or theological labels, are agreed that the source of evil in the world is external to Man. They view evil as rooted in the corruption of society. They believe that the solution to all Man's problems can be found in societal reform.

But such reforms do not transform the basic nature of people. You do not change people's basic nature by improving their environment. Changing their environment simply converts them into more sophisticated sinners.

The Humanist view is absolutely contrary to Scripture. The Word of God teaches that the source of evil is rooted within Man's fallen nature, and that it is Man, and not society, which needs to be changed (Genesis 8:21, Jeremiah 17:9-10 and Mark 7:20-23). The Word also teaches that the only way this change can take place is through the work of the Holy Spirit within those persons who put their faith in Jesus.

God is going to prove this point by using the Millennium like a great experimental laboratory. He is going to place Mankind in a perfect environment of peace and prosperity for a thousand years. Satan will be bound. Righteousness will abound.

Yet, at the end, when Satan is released, most people will rally to him when he calls the nations to rebellion against Jesus (Revelation 20:7-10). The Millennium will prove that what Man needs is not a new society but a new heart. ✤

Answers to Two Key Questions About the Millennium

Who will populate the earth during the Millennium?

Those who live to the end of the Tribulation and have accepted Jesus as their Lord and Savior will be allowed to enter the Millennium in the flesh (Matthew 25:3-46). This will be a very small number of people because most of those who place their faith in Jesus during the Tribulation will be martyred for their faith (Revelation 7:9-14). All surviving unbelievers will be consigned to death and to Hades (Luke 17:26-37).

The believers who go into the Millennium in the flesh will begin to propagate, and the population of the world will grow exponentially. The reason the growth will be so rapid is because life spans will be expanded and death will be curtailed.

Isaiah says that people will live as long as a tree (Isaiah 66:22) and there will no longer be infants who live only a few days (Isaiah 66:20). The implication of Isaiah's prophecy is that during the Millennium the life span of those in the flesh will be returned to what it was before the Noahic flood, when people lived 800 to 1000 years. If so, then by the end of the Millennium, the population of the earth could easily exceed the current seven billion.

Will the Millennium take place on this earth or on a new earth?

The Millennial reign of Jesus will take place on this earth, but the earth will be greatly changed in nature. The first earth, the earth of Adam and Eve, was perfect. There were no poisonous animals or plants. There were no meat-eating animals. There were no natural cataclysms like earthquakes, tsunamis, or hurricanes. Man and nature lived together in perfect harmony.

But when Man sinned, God placed a curse on the earth, and the nature of the earth was radically changed. Death entered the world. Nature turned against Mankind. This new earth, earth number two, existed until the time of Noah.

When the worldwide flood occurred, this second earth was "destroyed" (2 Peter 3:6) in the sense that it was radically changed again. The earth's vapor canopy collapsed, its land mass separated into continents, the earth tilted on its axis, and the pressure of the water forced the formation of new mountain ranges. We have been living on earth number three ever since.

When Jesus returns to reign, the earth will be radically changed once more. The change agents will be earthquakes and supernatural phenomena in the skies (Revelation 6:12-14). Every island will be moved (Revelation 16:18-20), every valley will be lifted up and every mountain lowered (Isaiah 40:4).The topography of Israel will be radically changed, with Jerusalem becoming the highest place on earth (Isaiah 2:2).

Questions:

1) It is the position of the Catholic church and most of the old mainline denominations that we are living in the Millennium today. After reading about the Millennium, do you think it is really possible to argue we are in the Millennium?

_____

2) There is a powerful passage in Joel 3 about the Second Coming and the Lord's millennial reign. Read Joel 3:9-21. Where does this passage say the Lord will dwell when He returns?

_____

3) Amos speaks of the Messiah returning like a roaring lion (Amos 1:2). Where does this verse say the Lord will speak from? Amos ends his book by prophesying about the agricultural abundance of the Millennium (Amos 9:13-15). Where does he say the Jewish people will be at that time?

_____

4) Obadiah speaks of the Second Coming and the Millennium in verses 15-18. What does he say will be the characteristic of Mount Zion?

_____

5) Micah speaks of the Millennium in chapter 4, verses 1-7. The first three verses are identical to Isaiah 2:2-4. Micah adds new information in verses 4-7. Where does he say the Lord will reign?

_____

6) Read Zephaniah 3:14-20. What points does he make about the Millennium?

_____

7) Read Zechariah 2:9-13. What does this passage tell you about the Millennium?

_____

8) Read Zechariah 8:1-8, 12-13. What did you learn from this passage about the Millennium?

_____

9) Ezekiel reveals that the name of Jerusalem in Hebrew will be changed at the beginning of the Millennium from *Yerushalayim* to *Yahweh-Shemmah*. Read Ezekiel 48:35 to find out the meaning of this new name. If Jesus is not returning to reign from Jerusalem, why would the name of the city be changed to something it does not mean?

_____

Lesson 20

Heaven

> **Fact:** *The Bible teaches that Heaven will be a tangible place located on a new earth.*

Key Scripture: *"For I consider that the sufferings of this present time are not worthy to be compared with the glory that is to be revealed to us"* (Romans 8:18).

Most Christians seem to believe that going to Heaven means being a disembodied spirit residing in an ethereal world, floating around on a cloud playing a harp. And to say the least, they can't seem to get excited about that picture.

The Bible tells us in great detail what the Millennium will be like, but it gives us almost no detailed information about Heaven, or what might be called the Eternal State. What it does tell us often comes as a great surprise to most Christians because the verses about Heaven have been so terribly spiritualized. For example, the Bible plainly says the Redeemed will live eternally on a new earth, not in an ethereal place called Heaven.

The New Earth

Isaiah was the first to speak of this truth when he spoke of "the new heavens and the new earth" which will endure forever before the Lord (Isaiah 66:22). This truth is repeated in the book of Revelation where the apostle John says he was shown a new earth, "for the first heaven and the first earth passed away" (Revelation 21:1).

John goes on to describe the new Jerusalem descending to the new earth, "coming down out of heaven from God" (Revelation 21:2). And then he states that God Himself will come to live on the new earth: "Behold, the tabernacle of God is among men, and He shall dwell among them, and they shall be His people, and God Himself shall be among them" (Revelation 21:3).

This truth had already been revealed to the Old Testament prophets. While being taken on a prophetic tour of the millennial temple, Ezekiel was told by his guide (the Lord Jesus in a pre-incarnate appearance): "Son of man, this is the place of My throne and the place of the soles of My feet, where I will dwell among the sons of Israel forever" (Ezekiel 43:7).

The Redeemed are going to dwell forever in new bodies on a new earth in a new Jerusalem in the presence of Almighty God and His Son, Jesus. Heaven will come to earth!

The New Jerusalem

The most detailed information which the Scriptures give about Heaven pertains to our eternal abode — the new Jerusalem. Twenty verses in Chapter 21 of Revelation are devoted to a description of it.

The information contained in

Revelation 21 is not the first reference in the Bible to the new Jerusalem. It is mentioned in Hebrews 11:10 as a city "whose architect and builder is God." Jesus made a reference to it that is recorded in John 14:1-4. He called it His "Father's house," and He said He would prepare a place in it for His Church.

The city is described in Revelation as beautifully decorated, like "a bride adorned for her husband" (Revelation 21:2). Later, John actually refers to the city as the bride of the Lamb (Revelation 21:9), because the city contains the bride of Christ, His Church.

This implies that at the end of the Millennium all the Redeemed will be taken off the present earth and placed in the new Jerusalem which will most likely be suspended in the heavens. From that vantage point we will watch as God burns up this earth and reshapes it like a hot ball of wax into a new earth, a perfected earth like the one which God created in the beginning. Then, we will be lowered down to that new earth inside the new Jerusalem.

The Size of the City

The city will be spectacular in both size and appearance. It will be in the form of a cube that is 1,500 miles in every direction! And it will reflect "the glory of God" (Revelation 21:11, 16).

The incredible size means the city would stretch from Canada to the Gulf of Mexico and from the Atlantic coast of America to Colorado. It would also extend 1,500 miles into the atmosphere.

This tremendous extension of the city vertically into the air is a clue that the new earth may be considerably larger than the current earth. Otherwise, the city would not be proportional to its surroundings.

It is likely that it will have vertical streets as well as horizontal ones because our glorified bodies, which we are told will be like the body of Jesus after his resurrection (Philippians 3:21), will be immune to the current laws of gravity.

The Beauty of the City

And what streets they will be! The Bible says they will be "pure gold, like transparent glass" (Revelation 21:21). In fact, the whole city will be made of pure gold with the appearance of clear glass (Revelation 21:18).

The city will sit on a foundation made of 12 layers of precious stones (Revelation 21:19-20). Each layer will feature the name of one of the 12 apostles (Revelation 21:14). The city will be surrounded by a jasper wall over 200 feet high (Revelation 21:17). There will be 12 gates, three on each side, and each one will be named for one of the tribes of Israel (Revelation 21:12).

And yes, the gates will be "pearly gates," each one consisting of one huge pearl (Revelation 21:21).

Best of all, God the Father and Jesus will both reside in the city with us (Revelation 21:22). The Shekinah glory of God will illuminate the city constantly, and thus there will be no night nor will there ever be any need for any type of artificial light or the light of the sun (Revelation 22:5).

The throne of God and His Son will be in the city, and "a river of the water of life, clear as crystal" will flow down the middle of the city's main street with the tree of life growing on both sides of the river, yielding 12 kinds of fruit — a different fruit each month (Revelation 22:1-2).

That's it. God's Word only gives us a glimpse of Heaven. But what a tantalizing glimpse it is! It's a scene of perfect peace and joy and beauty.

The Activities of Heaven

What will we do for eternity? Again, the Word is strangely silent. All it says is that we "shall serve Him" (Revelation 22:3).

We will probably spend a great deal of our time in worship, singing the psalms of King David, with him directing us. It is likely that our talents will be magnified, and we will be able to sing or paint or write with a majesty and scope we never imagined possible — and all to the glory of God!

Surely we will spend considerable time in the study of God's Word. Think of studying the Gospel of John with the apostle John as the teacher! Or imagine Jesus teaching the Old Testament, even as He did to His disciples following His resurrection (Luke 24:44-45). The Word of God is infinite in its depth, and I believe we will undoubtedly continue learning from it forever.

As we study the Word, we will grow in spiritual maturity in the likeness of Jesus. And since God is infinite, no matter how much we grow in His likeness, there will just be that much more growing ahead of us. In this regard, our spiritual growth will likely pick up where it left off in this life.

Perhaps the Lord will give us the opportunity to see "instant video replays" of great events in Bible history. And what about tours of the universe? Surely we will be able to travel through space in our glorified bodies and see the miracles of God's creation up close. Imagine visiting all the planets in our galaxy as well as touring thousands of other galaxies!

Reigning with Jesus

We are also told in Revelation 22:3 that we will serve God as His "bond-servants." This surely means we will be given productive work to do. What that work will be, the Scriptures do not say. But there is a hint in Revelation 22:5 where it says we will reign with the Lord "forever and ever."

To reign implies, of necessity, that we must reign over someone. Who will that be? Again, there is an intriguing clue. Revelation 21:24-27 refers to "nations" that will live on the new earth outside the new Jerusalem. Revelation 22:2 indicates that the people composing these nations will be in fleshly bodies, for it says that the leaves of the tree of life will be used for "the healing of the nations."

Who are these "nations"? This is one of the greatest mysteries of Bible prophecy. There are as many different guesses as there are commentaries on the book of Revelation.

Could they be the Redeemed who accept Jesus during the Millennium? Nothing is said about the ultimate destiny of those who are saved during the Millennium. No promises are made to them of glorified bodies.

Heavenly Fellowship

This brings us to the greatest blessing of Heaven. Revelation 22:4 says we shall see the face of God!

The Word says in Exodus 33:20 that no man has ever seen the face of God. But we will be given that privilege when we fellowship with Him in Heaven.

And that is really what Heaven is all about. We will experience an intimacy with the Lord that transcends anything possible in this life. We were created for fellowship with God (John 4:23), and that purpose will reach its zenith in the Eternal State as we live in God's presence. ✤

The Nature of the "New Earth"

Will the new eternal earth be completely new, or will it be this earth rejuvenated?

The Bible teaches that the present earth is eternal: "Generations come and generations go, but the earth remains forever" (Ecclesiastes 1:4; see also Psalm 78:69 and Psalm 148:6).

It is true that 2 Peter 3:10 says the current earth will be "destroyed with intense heat," but the same context says that the earth of Noah's time was "destroyed" by water (2 Peter 3:5-6). Noah's earth did not cease to exist, rather, it was "destroyed" in the sense that it was radically changed by the worldwide flood.

God loves His creation, and He is determined to restore it to its original perfection.

The promise of a redeemed and restored creation is reaffirmed in the New Testament. Peter referred to the promise in his second sermon at the Temple in Jerusalem. He told his audience that Jesus would remain in Heaven until the time comes for the "restoration of all things" (Acts 3:21).

Paul elaborates the theme in Romans 8:8-18. He declares that the whole creation is in "slavery to corruption" (verse 21). This is a reference to what physicists call the Second Law of Thermodynamics; namely, that all of creation is running down, moving from order to disorder — that all of creation is in bondage to decay.

Paul then pictures the creation as a pregnant woman waiting anxiously for the moment of delivery when the curse will be lifted and the creation will be redeemed. He says that will occur at "the revealing of the sons of God" (verse 19). That is a reference to the resurrection of the saints.

We are actually living on earth number four, as you will see from the chart on the next page.

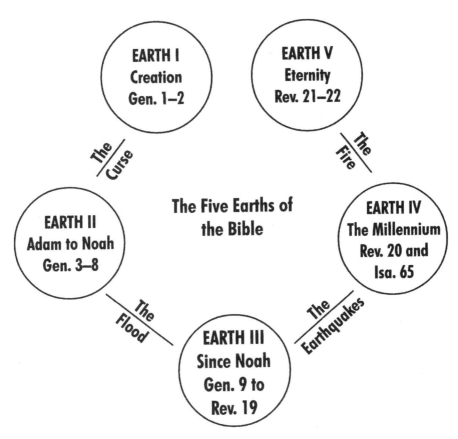

The Five Earths of the Bible

1) The original earth was created perfect (Genesis 1). It was corrupted by the sin of Man (Genesis 3:1-13) and the subsequent curse of God (Genesis 3:14-24), producing earth number 2.

2) The second earth was radically changed from the original. Natural cataclysms began, some animals became meat-eaters and a threat to Mankind, and some plants and animals became poisonous. People had to strive against nature to make their living. Due to the sin nature inherited from Adam, people began to rebel against God, and this revolt continued to increase until God decided to destroy the earth by water, producing earth number 3.

3) The third earth is the one we live on today. Its topography and atmosphere were radically changed by the flood. When Jesus returns, the earth will be radically changed once again through unprecedented earthquakes (Revelation 6:12-14 and 16:17-21), producing earth number 4.

4) The fourth earth, the earth of the Millennium, will become abundant once again with lush vegetation (Isaiah 30:23-26 and Amos 9:13-14). The Dead Sea will become alive (Ezekiel 47:1-9). Most important, the curse will be partially lifted, making it possible for Mankind to be reconciled to nature and for nature to be reconciled to itself.

5) At the end of the Millennium, the earth will be engulfed in fire and will be totally renovated and put back to its original perfection, producing the eternal earth where the Redeemed will live forever in the New Jerusalem.

Questions:

1) What is the most amazing thing you learned from this lesson?

_____

_____

2) Have you been clinging to this world because you had no idea what Heaven would be like?

_____

_____

3) If you have no zeal for God's Word or for fellowship with Him at a weekly church service, why do you think you would be happy in His presence eternally?

_____

_____

4) Many people spiritualize the description of the New Jerusalem in Revelation 21, arguing that it is a symbolic description of the Church. What do you think, and why?

_____

_____

5) Could you honestly endorse the following words of the Apostle Paul?

    a) "To live is Christ, and to die is gain" (Philippians 1:21). _____

    b) "I prefer rather to be absent from the body and to be at home with the Lord" (2 Corinthians 5:8). _____

6) If you were to die this very day, are you confident you would go to Heaven? If so, why?

_____

_____

_____

7) The most comprehensive and detailed book ever written about Heaven is one by Randy Alcorn that is simply titled, *Heaven* (Tyndale House, 2004). Here is a quote from the book: ". . . in order to get a picture of Heaven — which will one day be centered on the New Earth — you don't need to look up at the clouds; you need to look around you and imagine what all this world would be like without sin and death and suffering and corruption." Your response?

_____

_____

Lesson 21

Heavenly Rewards

Fact: *Believers will be judged of their works to determine their degrees of rewards.*

Key Scripture: *"For the Son of Man is going to come in the glory of His Father with His angels, and will then repay every man according to his deeds"* (Matthew 16:27).

A day will come when all believers will be judged of their works, not to determine their eternal destiny, but to ascertain their degrees of rewards (2 Corinthians 5:10 and Revelation 20:12).

We are not saved by our works (Ephesians 2:8-9), but we are saved to do good works (Ephesians 2:10 and Titus 2:14). All believers are given one or more spiritual gifts by the Holy Spirit at the time of their salvation, and they are expected to use those gifts to advance the Lord's kingdom on earth.

Believers will be judged not only on the quantity of their works, but also on their quality (1 Corinthians 3:13) and their motive (1 Corinthians 4:4-5). Some who are saved but who never used their spiritual gifts for the Lord, or who did so for the wrong motive (like personal glory), will have all their works burned up and will receive no special rewards beyond eternal life (1 Corinthians 3:15).

God's Memory

The Bible says in Malachi 3:16 that there is a Book of Remembrance in which God has written down all the things we have done for Him. Most of these things we have forgotten, but not God. Jesus said we would even be rewarded for giving a person a cup of cold water (Matthew 10:41-42)! Hebrews 6:10 says that "God is not unjust so as to forget your work and the love you have shown toward His name, in having ministered and in still ministering to the saints." Once again, we are assured that God will never forget any of our good works.

As to the specific rewards, there is a great variety of them mentioned in the Scriptures. These include special crowns (1 Corinthians 9:24-25) and robes (Revelation 19:8), heavenly treasures (Matthew 6:19), levels of glory (Romans 8:18) and degrees of reigning responsibility (Luke 19:11-27).

Various Crowns

The Bible teaches there are five different types of crowns that will be rewarded to believers.

1) The Victor's Crown (1 Corinthians 9:24-25) — This crown will be given to those who showed exceptional self-discipline in their service to the Lord, always putting His will before their own.

2) The Soul Winner's Crown (1 Thessalonians 2:19) — This crown will be bestowed upon those who were involved in soul winning — including evangelists, Bible teachers, personal witnessers and those who financed their efforts.

3) The Crown of Righteousness (2 Timothy 4:8) — This crown will be rewarded to those who lived their lives longing for the Lord's return — those who lived with an eternal perspective.

4) The Shepherd's Crown (1 Peter 5:4) — This is the reward for faithful pastors and elders.

5) The Crown of Life (James 1:2) — This reward is reserved for those who persevered under trial — those who endured difficult trials, temptations, suffering, persecution and even martyrdom. Jesus mentioned this reward specifically in Revelation 2:10.

Heavenly Treasure

The Bible says the redeemed will receive different amounts of treasure in Heaven. Jesus Himself made this promise in Matthew 6:9 when He said: "Do not store up for yourself treasures on earth where moths and vermin destroy and where thieves break in and steal, but store up for yourself treasures in Heaven . . ."

The Apostle Paul mentions the same reward in 1 Timothy 6:17-19. Here he tells Timothy to instruct believers "to do good" and "to be rich in good works" and "generous to share," for by doing so, they are "storing up for themselves the treasures of a good foundation for the future."

Levels of Glory

The Scriptures also assure us that there will be distinctions of glory that will be given to believers. Consider these words of Paul: "For I consider that the sufferings of this present time

are not worthy to be compared with the glory that is to be revealed to us" (Romans 8:18). Paul speaks of this type of reward again in 2 Corinthians 4:17 where he writes: "For momentary, light affliction is producing for us an eternal weight of glory far beyond all comparison . . ."

What all this means is not precisely spelled out in any detail, but the possibilities are mind-boggling. So much so, that when we experience it, we may well find ourselves wishing that we had been given more opportunities to suffer for the Lord!

Degrees of Reigning Authority

Another type of reward mentioned in the Bible is one that relates to both the Millennium and the Eternal State, It is the degree of reigning authority we will share with Jesus under His oversight.

We are assured that we will reign with Him (2 Timothy 2:12 and Revelation 5:9-10). But our degree of participation in His reign will be related to our service to Him now (Luke 19: 1-27). Some will reign over one city, some over five and some over none.

Attitudes Toward Rewards

Unfortunately, most Christians seem to have a very cavalier attitude toward rewards, and there are several reasons for this lack of concern.

First, many seem to think that if they are motivated by a reward, they will lose the reward! This strange attitude is based on a teaching of Jesus that is recorded in Matthew 6:1-4. In this passage, Jesus warns His disciples "not to practice your righteousness in front of others to be seen by them" because "if you do, you will have no reward from your Father in heaven."

What Jesus is warning against is doing our good works in order to receive the praise of people. He is saying that we should be motivated instead for the praise of God. We are supposed to be motivated by the hope that when we stand before Jesus to be judged, He will say, "Well done, good and faithful servant" (Matthew 25:21).

A second reason some believers are not passionate about rewards is because they believe they will be temporary. This attitude is based on a scene in Heaven that is described by the Apostle John in Revelation 4. John says he saw 24 elders worshiping God (Revelation 4:10-11). As part of their worship, they kneel and cast their crowns before God's throne.

This scene has produced a teaching that as soon as we receive our rewards in Heaven, we will cast them at the feet of Jesus and be done with them. They are, therefore, viewed as no big deal.

But Revelation 4:9 presents a qualifying word. It says that the 24 elders do this "whenever" (NIV) worship occurs. That does not indicate a once and for all action. In Revelation 5:4 we are told that the crowns "will never fade away."

A Socialist View of Rewards

Some argue the rewards have to be temporary because there can be no distinctions in Heaven, otherwise there would be jealousy, and such a sin cannot exist in the perfect atmosphere of Heaven. But this is an earthly view. In Heaven, our sin nature will not exist. We will live in perfect love.

Thus, when we see a saint wearing a special crown or exhibiting some other reward, our hearts will be filled with admiration and appreciation — the same as we feel in this life when one of our children receives a special reward.

Pastor Glenn Meredith of McKinney, Texas, who has taught extensively about heavenly rewards, has concluded: "Believe me, there will be eternal distinctions in Heaven because what you do now in this life will have a profound impact on the rewards you will receive and the services you will be assigned."

> *"Rejoice and be glad, for your reward in heaven is great . . ."* (Words of Jesus in Matthew 5:12). ✤

Questions:

1) Since our heavenly rewards are going to be based in part on how we used our spiritual gifts, do you know what your spiritual gifts are? Read Romans 12:6-8, 1 Corinthians 12:4-11,28-31, Ephesians 4:11 and 1 Peter 4:10-11). List below the spiritual gifts you think you have been given by the Holy Spirit. If you are in a Bible study group, read the list to them and then ask them if they can identify other gifts that you may not be aware of.

_____

_____

2) Did you know there are tests on the Internet that can help you identify your spiritual gifts? Just Google "spiritual gifts tests." Take a couple of these tests and then write below the gifts you have that were identified by these tests.

_____

_____

3) What heavenly reward would you most like to receive and why?

_____

_____

_____

4) Do you feel like you fully understand the Bible's teaching that we are saved by grace and not by works (Ephesians 2:8-9), but we are saved for good works (Ephesians 2:10 and Titus 2:14)? What do you think is the meaning of this for cultural Christians who are lackadaisical about practicing their faith?

_____

_____

_____

_____

5) Give some thought to the rewards that believers receive in this life as a result of their faith in Jesus as Lord and Savior and the gift of the Holy Spirit residing within them. List some of those rewards below:

_____

_____

_____

_____

6) Due to the significance that the Scriptures give to heavenly rewards, do you feel like you will now be more motivated to earn some of the rewards by serving the Lord more diligently?

_____

_____

_____

Lesson 22

Signs of the Times

> **Fact:** *We are given signs to watch for that will indicate the season of the Lord's return.*

Key Scripture: *". . . when these things* [prophesied end times events] *begin to take place, straighten up and lift up your heads, because your redemption is drawing near"* (Luke 21: 28).

There are no signs for the Rapture. It can occur at any moment. But the Bible teaches that we can know the season of the Second Coming and the period immediately preceding it — the Tribulation.

Knowing the Season

The reason we can know the season of the Tribulation and the Second Coming is because the Bible is full of signs which will signal the season of the Lord's return, and we are told to watch for them. These signs are found in both the Old and New Testaments, and there are a great number of them.

For example, one out of every 25 verses in the New Testament specifically concerns the Second Coming. But what is not so well known is the fact that there are hundreds of prophecies in the Old Testament which also relate to the Second Coming.

In addition to the Major and Minor Prophets, the Psalms are full of Messianic prophecies regarding the Lord's return. In fact, Psalm 2 is one of the most important Second Coming prophecies in the Bible.

An Area of Ignorance

Many, if not most, Christians have ignored the study of these signs because they believe that since "Jesus is coming like a thief in the night," it is a waste of time to try to interpret the signs to anticipate the time of His coming.

It is true that Jesus said He would come like a thief in the night (Matthew 24:42-43). But Paul later explained that Jesus meant this statement for non-believers, not for Christians.

Paul makes this point in his first letter to the Thessalonians. In chapter 5 he says that although Jesus is coming back like a thief in the night, there is no reason for His return to surprise any Christian (1 Thessalonians 5:4). Why not? Because, as Paul puts it, "Brethren, you are not in darkness, that the day should overtake you like a thief; for you are all sons of light and sons of day" (1 Thessalonians 5:4-5).

What does Paul mean by this seemingly enigmatic statement? He was referring to the fact the when we accept Jesus as our Savior, we are given the indwelling presence of the Holy Spirit (Romans 5:5). Through the Spirit we receive the power to become spiritually enlightened.

So, Paul is saying in 1 Thessalonians 5 that we can know the season of the Lord's return because we have been given spiritual discernment through the gift of the Holy Spirit.

Jesus' Concept

In Matthew 24, Jesus compared the signs of His return to the signs of a pregnancy. Think of it this way: You may not know the date when a pregnant woman is to deliver, but sooner or later, as you watch the development of her pregnancy, you will think to yourself, "That baby is going to be born soon!" Why? You can tell by looking.

Jesus said the signs pointing to His return would be like "birth pangs" (Matthew 24:8). Any birth mother knows what Jesus meant by this remark. As the time nears for His return, the signs will increase in frequency and intensity, just like birth pangs. For example, there will be more earthquakes and more intense ones.

This is a crucial point that is usually overlooked. Thus, people often scoff at the signs by saying, "There have always been wars and rumors of wars and earthquakes and famines." Yes, there have always been such calamities, but they are now increasing in frequency and intensity, just as Jesus prophesied.

In Hebrews 10:25 we are told that we are to "encourage one another; and all the more, as you see the day drawing near." The context is the Second Coming of Jesus. This passage makes it clear that we can know the season of the Lord's return — that tangible things will be visible to alert us to the Lord's soon return. What are those things? What are the signs the Bible tells us to watch for?

The Signs of the Times

There are a great number and variety of these signs. In fact, there are so many that it is difficult to get a handle on them. The best way to get a grasp on them is to group them into several broad categories. Let's take a look at them in that manner.

1) The Signs of Nature — The signs pertaining to nature are the ones that are least respected. The problem is twofold. First, people are prone to think, "There have always been earthquakes, volcanic eruptions, hurricanes and famines. So, what else is new?"

The second problem is more philosophical. We are a very rationalistic people and, as such, we tend to be skeptical of the supernatural. If we can't see it, weigh it and measure it, we can't accept its existence. Yet, the Bible teaches there is a whole realm of reality that is not normally perceptible to the senses — the realm of the supernatural that includes angels and demons (Ephesians 6:10-12).

Because we are so rationalistic, we tend to scoff at the idea that God would speak to us through signs of nature. But the Bible affirms this over and over. The Old Testament prophets repeatedly pointed to signs of nature and claimed that they indicated the judgment of God or His impending wrath.

Today we are seeing natural calamities increase in frequency and intensity, just as prophesied.

2) The Signs of Society — Jesus said He would return at a time when society would resemble "the days of Noah" (Matthew 24:37). The Old Testament tells us that Noah's time was one of immorality and violence because the thoughts of men's hearts were continually focused on evil (Genesis 6:5-13).

The Apostle Paul emphasized this sign in his writing. In 2 Timothy 3:1-5, Paul says that the society of the end times will be characterized by great stress. It will be a society in which people will love three things: self, money and pleasure (2 Timothy 3:2-4). What Paul identifies here is the religion, the god, and the lifestyle of the end time society: Humanism, Materialism and Hedonism.

Paul describes the resulting despair in graphic terms: "men will be . . . boastful, arrogant, revilers, disobedient to parents, ungrateful, unholy, unloving, irreconcilable, malicious gossips, without self-control, brutal, haters of good, treacherous, reckless, conceited . . ." (2 Timothy 3:2-4). Needless to say, this reads like the evening news here in America.

3) The Spiritual Signs — There are numerous spiritual signs that we are to watch for, both negative and positive ones.

The negative ones are very negative indeed. They include such things as the appearance of false Christs and their cultic groups (Matthew 24:5,11, 24), the apostasy of the professing Church (2 Timothy 3:5), the persecution of faithful Christians (Luke 21:12-19) and an outbreak of Satanism (1 Timothy 4:1).

We are in the midst of the fulfillment of all these prophecies. Much of mainline Christianity is wallowing in apostasy. Cultic groups are multiplying. Christians are being persecuted worldwide.

But, thankfully, there are some very positive spiritual signs that are prophesied for the end times. One is the proclamation of the Gospel to all the world (Matthew 24:14).

This prophecy began to be fulfilled in the 20th Century as a result of modern technology such as shortwave radio and satellite television. With the advent of computer technology, the Bible has been rapidly translated into hundreds, even thousands, of languages and dialects.

Another positive sign is the increasing understanding of Bible prophecy. Many of the prophecies concerning the end times were not even understood by the prophet who gave them. A good example is Daniel. He was mystified by many of the end time prophecies which the Lord gave him. When he complained about this, the Lord told him to stop worrying about it because "the words are concealed and sealed up until the end time" (Daniel 12:4,9).

As we get nearer to the day the Lord will return, we understand more and more of Bible prophecy. Some of the new understanding is due to the development of world events, such as the re-establishment of the nation of Israel. Other mysterious prophecies can now be understood due to modern technological developments.

One of the most glorious spiritual signs is the great outpouring of God's Spirit that the Church is receiving in these end times. The Bible prophesies that a great Holy Spirit empowerment will come in the latter days to enable Christians who are open to the Spirit's power to stand against the assaults of Satan.

In Joel 2:23 this is put in the imagery of an "early rain and a latter rain." The early rain was at Pentecost and continued through the early history of the Church when it was young and struggling to get established. The latter rain is occurring today as the true Church stands against the final assaults of Satan.

4) The Signs of Technology — The explosion of scientific knowledge and its technical application to communications, transportation, data processing and weapons of war is definitely a sign of the soon return of the Lord (Daniel 12:4).

For example, how could all the people of the world be given the mark of the beast (Revelation 13:16-18) before the invention of lasers and computers? How could the False Prophet make an image of the Antichrist that would appear to be alive (Revelation 13:14-15) before the development of robotics and holograms?

5) The Signs of World Politics — Bible prophecy forecasts the coming together of a certain international pattern of nations in the end times.

The nation of Israel will once again exist, and all the nations of the world will seek to destroy the Jewish state (Zechariah 12:1-3). Particularly menacing to Israel will be a superpower located in "the remote parts of the north" (Ezekiel 38:6). This nation is identified in Ezekiel 38 in terms that can only be interpreted to mean modern day Russia.

The existence of the Jewish state will also be threatened by its Arab neighbors (Psalm 83 and Ezekiel 35).

The resurgence of China as a superpower is also prophesied (Revelation 9:12-16 and 16:12), as is the reunification of Europe (Daniel 7:7-8, 24).

The world will be characterized by wars and rumors of wars (Matthew 24:6). The nations will also be afflicted with internal political strife that will often lead to "kingdom against kingdom," or civil war (Matthew 24:7).

Lawlessness will increase everywhere (Matthew 24:12), a prophecy that has been fulfilled on the international scene with the advent of modern terrorism.

6) The Signs of Israel — The most important group of signs, more important than all the rest put together, is the group that pertains to the nation of Israel. One reason is because end time prophecy focuses on Israel.

Another reason Israel is so important is because the Jewish people are God's prophetic time clock. This means that very often when God is revealing an important event that will take place in the future, He will point to the Jewish people and assert that when a certain thing happens to them, the important event will also occur.

An example of this principle is found in Luke 21:24 where Jesus told His disciples to watch Jerusalem. His point was that Jerusalem would be conquered and then "trampled under foot by the Gentiles" until it was time for Him to return. In other words, He was saying that whenever the Jews win back the city of Jerusalem from the Gentiles, it will be a sure sign that His return is near.

The Romans were in control of Jerusalem when Jesus spoke these words. They were succeeded by many nations and empires until June 7, 1967, when the Jews finally regained sovereignty over the city of Jerusalem for the first time in 1,897 years.

The Super Sign

There is a decisive "super sign" that overshadows all the ones mentioned above and which clearly indicates that Jesus is at the very gate of Heaven preparing for His soon return.

That sign is what could be called CONVERGENCE. What it means is that for the first time in history, all the end times signs of the Lord's return have converged. None are missing.

This means we are living on borrowed time, and the crucial question for all of us is, "Are you ready for the Lord's return?" ✤

Questions:

1) How do you feel about the "super sign"? Do you think we are truly living in the times when all the signs have converged?

_____

_____

2) Read Revelation 11:3-11 concerning the two witnesses of God who will preach in Jerusalem during the first half of the Tribulation. What is it about verses 8-11 that could not be understood in natural terms before the 1960s?

_____

_____

3) Read 2 Timothy 3:1-5. Does this sound like a description of our nation today?

_____

_____

4) In the early 1900s, when C. I. Scofield was preparing the publication of his famous study Bible which was published in 1909, he made the following comment about Ezekiel 38 and 39: "These chapters picture an end times invasion of Israel by Russia and certain allies. I don't understand it, and I cannot explain it, but I believe it because the Bible says it will happen." Why were the prophecies in these chapters so difficult to understand then, but not today?

_____

_____

5) One of the negative spiritual signs of the end times is presented in 1 Timothy 4:1. Can you name some fulfillments of this prophecy in America today?

_____

_____

Lesson 23

Death

Fact: *Very few believers are aware of what the Bible teaches about life after death.*

Key Scripture: *"The last enemy that will be abolished is death"* (1 Corinthians 15:26).

Are you ready for the Lord's return? What if you die before He returns? Are you ready to face death? Can you say with confidence that after you take your last breath, you will be in the presence of the Lord?

And do you know what happens to people when they die? Do believers go to a place called Purgatory where they are tormented in order to purify them for Heaven? Do unbelievers go straight to Hell? Do believers become angels and unbelievers demons?

The Bible says that most people live in lifelong bondage to the fear of death (Hebrews 2:15). Most of the time that fear is suppressed, but it is always there, just below the surface. It normally surfaces when a friend or family member dies, when a person experiences a near-death event like a serious auto accident or when a person begins to reach middle age. And, of course, crouching in a fox hole with bombs exploding all around always gives rise to thoughts of death!

Events at Death

So, what happens when you die? If you are a child of God, your spirit is immediately ushered into the bosom of Jesus by His holy angels. Your spirit remains in Heaven, in the presence of God, until the time of the Rapture.

When Jesus comes for His Church, He brings your spirit with Him, resurrects and glorifies your body, making it eternal in nature (1 Corinthians 15 and 1 Thessalonians 4). You reign with Jesus for a thousand years and then live eternally with Him on the new earth (Revelation 20-22).

If you are not a child of God, then your spirit goes to Hades at your death. This is a place of torments where your spirit is held until the resurrection of the unrighteous which takes place at the end of the millennial reign of Jesus.

At that resurrection you are taken before the Great White Throne of God where you are judged by your works and then condemned to the "second death," which is the "lake of fire" or Hell (Revelation 20:11-15).

The Intermediate State

Some of the greatest confusion about life after death relates to the intermediate state between death and eternity. Some people advocate a concept called "soul sleep." They argue that both the saved and unsaved are unconscious after death until the return of Jesus.

But the Bible makes it crystal clear that our spirit does not lose its consciousness at death. The only thing that "falls asleep" is our body — in a symbolic sense.

Paul says in 2 Corinthians 5:8 that he would prefer to be "absent from the body and at home with the Lord." In Philippians 1:21 he observes, "For me to live is Christ and to die is gain." He then adds in verse 23 that his desire is "to depart and be with Christ." Paul certainly did not expect to be in a coma after he died!

If then our spirits retain their consciousness after death, where do they go? The Bible teaches that prior to the resurrection of Jesus, the spirits of the dead went to a place called Hades ("Sheol" in the Old Testament). The spirits existed there consciously in one of two compartments, either Paradise or Torments. This concept is pictured graphically in Jesus' story of the rich man and Lazarus (Luke 16: 19-31).

The reason the saved went to Paradise in Hades instead of Heaven is because their sins were covered by their faith but not forgiven. Therefore, they could not be ushered into the presence of the Holy Father. The Bible teaches that "without the shedding of blood there is no forgiveness" (Hebrews 9:22 and Leviticus 17:11).

The forgiveness of their sins had to await the sacrifice of a perfect person who would die for their sins and not His own. That person was Jesus (2 Corinthians 5:21 and 1 Peter 2:24).

The Bible indicates that after the death of Jesus on the Cross, He descended into Hades to declare the good news that He had shed His blood for the sins of Mankind (1 Peter 3:18-19 and 4:6). The Bible also indicates that after His resurrection, when He ascended into Heaven, Jesus took Paradise with Him, transferring the spirits of dead saints from Hades to Heaven (Ephesians 4:8-9 and 2 Corinthians 12:1-4). The spirits of dead saints are thereafter pictured as being in Heaven before the throne of God (See Revelation 6:9 and 7:9).

Our Bodies

After death there will never be a time when we will exist without a body. We will never be ethereal spirits!

Those of us who are saved are destined to have two future bodies. We will first receive an intermediate spirit body — intermediate between our current fleshly body and our future glorified body.

The evidence of such a body is found several places in Scripture:

- 1 Samuel 28 — When Samuel, who was dead, appeared to Saul and the Witch of Endor.

- Matthew 17 — When Moses and Elijah appeared at the Transfiguration of Jesus.

- Luke 16 — When the Rich Man and Lazarus are portrayed in Hades.

- Revelation 7 — When the Tribulation Martyrs are pictured standing before the throne of God in white robes.

Our second future body will be received at the time of our resurrection, which for current day believers will be at the time of the Rapture.

At that time, if we have died

previously, our current bodies will be resurrected and glorified. And if we are alive, our bodies will suddenly be translated from mortal to immortal.

All this is described in 1 Thessalonians 4:13-18 where the Apostle Paul describes a series of events that will happen at the time of the Rapture:

- A trumpet will blow and an archangel will shout.

- Jesus will appear in the heavens, bringing with Him the spirits of the dead Church Age saints.

- He will resurrect their bodies, reunite their spirits with their bodies, and then glorify their bodies.

- He will then catch up all living believers, converting their bodies from mortal to immortal on the way up.

The glorified body we will receive at the time of our resurrection will be our body for eternity. This raises the question, "What is a glorified body?"

The Glorified Body

Paul describes it in 1 Corinthians 15:42-44. He says our bodies are buried as "perishable" and raised as "imperishable." They are "sown in dishonor" and "raised in glory." They are "sown in weakness" and "raised in power." He concludes by saying, "if there is a natural body, there is also a spiritual body." Notice the key words:

- Imperishable — Eternal

- Glorious — Perfected

- Powerful — Victorious over Sin

- Spiritual — Subjected totally to the Holy Spirit

Those who are glorified will never again be subject to disease, pain, suffering and death. Their bodies will be perfected, and therefore, the lame will walk, the deaf will hear, the blind will see, the mute will speak and those with dementia will have their minds cleared.

Perhaps the best way to think about a glorified body is to think of the body of Jesus after His resurrection. It is described in Philippians 3:

20) . . . We eagerly wait for a Savior, the Lord Jesus Christ;

21) who will transform the body of our humble state into conformity with the body of His glory, by the exertion of the power that He has even to subject all things to Himself.

So, according to this passage, our glorified body will be like Jesus' resurrection body. It will be tangible and recognizable. But it will have a different dimension to it because the body of Jesus could suddenly appear and disappear and could travel instantly from one place to another.

Questions

One of the most common questions people ask about life after death is, "Will we know each other in Heaven?" The answer is yes. And it can easily be derived through logic. Just think: If you are John or Betty in this life and you are saved, but you become someone else in Heaven, then John and Betty were not saved.

Another common question is whether or not we will eat in our glorified bodies. And again, the answer is yes. We know this for certain because Jesus ate several meals with His disciples in His glorified body after His resurrection (Luke 24:42-43 and John 21:10-15).

A very serious question is whether or not we will be able to sin in our glorified bodies. After all, Heaven's perfection did not prevent Satan from sinning. Jesus promised in Revelation 21:4 that in Heaven "there will be no more death or mourning or crying or pain . . ." Since "the wages of sin is death" (Romans 6:23), the promise of no more death is a promise of no more sin.

Our sin nature will be gone, replaced by the righteousness of Christ (Romans 5:19). Yes, it is true that Adam and Eve had no sin nature when they were created, and yet they sinned. But they had not been made righteous by Christ, and those who are now believers have been.

Randy Alcorn, who has written the most exhaustive book about Heaven, has summed up the answer to this vital question with these words:

> Once we become what the sovereign God has made us to be in Christ, and once we see Him as He is, then we'll see all things — including sin — for what they are. God won't need to restrain us from it. Sin will have absolutely no appeal. It will be, literally, unthinkable.

Maranatha! ✤

Questions:

1) What was the most surprising thing that you discovered in this lesson?

_____

_____

2) How do you feel about the following quotation from Randy Alcorn's book about Heaven? "Death is an abnormal condition because it tears apart what God created and joined together [body and soul]. God intended for our bodies to last as long as our souls . . . We are unified beings. That's why the bodily resurrection of the dead is so vital. And that's why Job rejoiced that in his flesh he would see God (Job 19:26)."

_____

_____

3) Are you afraid of death? Do you want to be assured of triumph over death? Then place your faith in Jesus as your Lord and Savior. You can do that by sincerely praying: "Heavenly Father, I confess to you that I am a sinner. I am sorry for my sins, and I desire they be forgiven by placing my faith in your Son, Jesus, as my Lord and Savior. I believe in faith that You have heard this prayer, and You have answered it, and I rejoice that I have been born again into Your eternal family. In Jesus' name, Amen." After you have said this prayer, seek out a Bible-believing church where you can witness your faith in a public confession of Jesus and in baptism. Then, get involved in a Bible study where you can grow in God's Word.

Lesson 24

A Summary Overview

> **Fact:** *The message of Bible prophecy for believers is that "Jesus will triumph, and we will win in the end!"*

Key Scripture: *"Thanks be to God, who gives us the victory through our Lord Jesus Christ"* (1 Corinthians 15: 57).

We have learned from God's Word that when those of us who are Christians die, our spirits never lose their consciousness (Philippians 1:21-23 and 2 Corinthians 5:8). Instead, our fully conscious spirits are immediately ushered into the presence of Jesus by His holy angels (Luke 16: 22).

Our spirits are clothed in an intermediate spirit body and remain in the Lord's presence until He appears for His Church at the time of the Rapture. At that time, He brings our spirits with Him, resurrects our bodies, reunites our spirits with our bodies, and then glorifies our bodies, perfecting them and rendering them eternal (1 Thessalonians 4:13-18).

We return with Him to Heaven in our glorified bodies where we are judged for our works to determine our degrees of rewards (2 Corinthians 5: 10). When this judgment is completed, we participate in a glorious wedding feast to celebrate the union of Jesus and His Bride, the Church (Revelation 19:7-9).

Witnesses of Glory

At the conclusion of the feast, we burst from the heavens with Jesus, returning with Him to the earth in glory (Revelation 19:14). We witness His victory at Armageddon, we shout "Hallelujah!" as He is crowned King of kings and Lord of lords, and we revel in His glory as He begins to reign over all the earth from Mt. Zion in Jerusalem (Zechariah 14:1-9 and Revelation 19:17-21).

For a thousand years we participate in that reign, assisting Him with the instruction, administration and enforcement of His perfect laws (Daniel 7:13-14,18,27 and Revelation 20:1-6). We see the earth regenerated and nature reconciled (Isaiah 11:6-9). We see holiness abound and the earth flooded with peace, righteousness and justice (Micah 4:1-7).

At the end of the Millennium we witness the release of Satan to deceive the nations. We see the truly despicable nature of the heart of Man as millions rally to Satan in his attempt to overthrow the throne of Jesus. But we will shout "Hallelujah!" again when we witness God's supernatural destruction of Satan's armies and see Satan himself cast into Hell where he will be tormented forever (Revelation 20:7-10).

We will next witness the Great White Throne Judgment when the unrighteous are resurrected to stand before God. We will see perfect holiness and justice in action as God pronounces His terrible judgment upon this congregation of the damned who have rejected His gift of love and mercy in Jesus Christ (Revelation 20:11-13).

Jesus will be fully vindicated as every knee shall bow and every tongue confess that He is Lord. Then the unrighteous will receive their just reward as they are cast into Hell (Revelation 20:14-15).

Witnesses of a New Creation

We will then witness the most spectacular fireworks display in all of history.

We will be taken to the New Jerusalem — the eternal mansion prepared by Jesus for His Bride — and from there we will watch as God renovates this earth with fire, burning away all the filth and pollution left by Satan's last revolt (2 Peter 3:12-13).

Just as the angels rejoiced when God created the universe, we will rejoice as we watch God superheat this earth and reshape it like a hot ball of wax into the New Earth, the eternal earth, the paradise where we will live forever in the presence of God (Revelation 21:1-7).

What a glorious moment it will be when we are lowered to the New Earth inside the fabulous New Jerusalem (Revelation 21:2). God will come down from Heaven to dwell with us (Revelation 21:3). He will proclaim: "Behold, I make all things new" (Revelation 21:5).

We will see God face to face (Revelation 22:4). He will wipe away all our tears (Revelation 21:4). Death will be no more (Revelation 21:4). We will be given new names (Revelation 2:17), and we will exist as individual personalities encased in perfect bodies (Philippians 3:21). And we will grow eternally in knowledge and love of our infinite Creator, honoring Him with our talents and gifts.

To say the least, these are promises of God that should give us hope. We should be able to get excited about them and desire to share them with those who do not know Jesus as their Lord and Savior. ✢

Quotation:

"A continual looking forward to the eternal world is not (as some modern people think) a form of escapism or wishful thinking, but one of the things a Christian is meant to do. It does not mean that we are to leave the present world as it is. If you read history you will find that the Christians who did most for the present world were just those who thought most of the next. The Apostles themselves, who set on foot the conversion of the Roman Empire, the great men who built up the Middle Ages, the English Evangelicals who abolished the Slave Trade, all left their mark on Earth, precisely because their minds were occupied with Heaven. It is since Christians have largely ceased to think of the other world that they have become so ineffective in this. Aim at Heaven and you will get earth 'thrown in:' aim at earth and you will get neither." C. S. Lewis in *Mere Christianity*.

Questions:

1) Do you understand now why a study of Bible prophecy is so important? What do you think is the most important reason?

_____

2) Do you desire to dig deeper into God's Prophetic Word? If so, consider the recommendations for further study on pages 109-110. Is there a particular subject that you want to find out more information about?

_____

3) Looking back over the lessons in this book, which one was the most interesting to you, and why?

_____

_____

4) Many people, including some pastors, like to joke that they are neither Amillennial, Premillennial nor Postmillennial. Instead, they say they are "Pan-millennial" because they don't know what is going to happen in the future, but they believe "it will all pan-out in the end." Do you see that this is just an excuse for not studying Bible prophecy? And do you realize now how much of God's Word they are ignoring? What would be your response to a Pan-millennialist?

_____

_____

_____

5) Many Christians ignore Bible prophecy because they say it is "too scary." As a result, many have never even read the book of Revelation. How would you respond to such a person?

_____

_____

6) Many pastors ignore the teaching and preaching of Bible prophecy because they say it is just pie-in-the-sky without any relevance to the here-and-now. Your response?

_____

_____

Recommendations for Further Study

Lesson 1: The Importance of Prophecy — Tim LaHaye and Ed Hindson, editors, *Exploring Bible Prophecy from Genesis to Revelation* (Eugene, OR: Harvest House, 2011). Also: A video program by David R. Reagan, *Fundamentals of Bible Prophecy* (Lamb & Lion Ministries, 1998).

Lesson 2: The Abuse of Prophecy — Paul Lee Tan, *The Interpretation of Prophecy* (Dallas, TX: Paul Lee Tan Ministries, 2010).

Lesson 3: The Varieties of Prophecy — Ada R. Habershon, *Study of the Types* (Grand Rapids, MI: Kregel Publications, 1974).

Lesson 4: The Interpretation of Prophecy — Tim LaHaye, *Understanding Bible Prophecy for Yourself* (Eugene, OR: Harvest House, 2009).

Lesson 5: End Time Viewpoints — Paul N. Benware, *Understanding End Times Prophecy* (Chicago, IL: Moody Press, 1995).

Lesson 6: Old Testament Prophecy — Leon J. Wood, *The Prophets of Israel* (Schaumburg, IL: Regular Baptist Press, 1979). Also: Nathan Jones and Steve Howell, *12 Faith Journeys of the Minor Prophets* (McKinney, TX: Lamb & Lion Ministries, 2016).

Lesson 7: Messianic Prophecy — David R. Reagan, *Jesus: The Lamb and the Lion* (McKinney, TX: Lamb & Lion Ministries, 2011).

Lesson 8: Two Cornerstone Prophecies — Renald E. Showers, *The Most High God: A Commentary on the Book of Daniel* (Bellmawr, NJ: The Friends of Israel Gospel Ministry, 1982).

Lesson 9: The Jews in Prophecy — David R. Reagan, *Israel in Bible Prophecy: Past, Present & Future* (McKinney, TX: Lamb & Lion Ministries, 2017).

Lesson 10: Replacement Theology — David R. Reagan, *The Jewish People: Rejected or Beloved?* (Lamb & Lion Ministries, 2014).

Lesson 11: New Testament Prophecy — David R. Reagan, *The Christ in Prophecy Study Guide* (McKinney, TX: Lamb & Lion Ministries, 2nd edition, 2001).

Lesson 12: The Church in Prophecy — John F. Walvoord, *The Church in Prophecy: Exploring God's Purpose for the Present Age* (Grand Rapids, MI: Kregel, revised edition, 1999).

Lesson 13: A Chronology of End Time Events — Ron Rhodes, *The End Times in Chronological Order* (Eugene, OR: Harvest House, 2012).

Lesson 14: The Rapture — Ed Hindson and Mark Hitchcock, *Can We Still Believe in the Rapture?* (Eugene, OR: Harvest House, 2017).

Lesson 15: The Tribulation — Tim LaHaye, *Revelation Illustrated and Made Plain* (Grand Rapids, MI: Zondervan Publishing House, 1975). David R. Reagan, *Wrath and Glory: Unveiling the Majestic Book of Revelation* (Green Forest, AR:

New Leaf Press, 2001). Second edition in 2016 by Lamb & Lion Ministries.

Lesson 16: The Antichrist — David R. Reagan, *The Man of Lawlessness* (McKinney, TX: Lamb & Lion Ministries, 2012).

Lesson 17: The Wars of the End Times — David R. Reagan, "The Wars of the End Times, *Lamplighter* magazine, September-October, 2009, pp. 3-7. Also available in a video edition by the same name (Lamb & Lion Ministries, 2015).

Lesson 18: The Second Coming — H. L. Willmington, *The King is Coming* (Wheaton, IL: Tyndale House Publishers, 1991).

Lesson 19: The Millennium — John F. Walwoord, *The Millennial Kingdom*, (Grand Rapids, MI: Zondervan Publishing House 1959).

Lesson 20: Heaven — Randy Alcorn, *Heaven* (Wheaton, IL: Tyndale House Publishers, 2004).

Lesson 21: Heavenly Rewards — Erwin W. Lutzer, *Your Eternal Reward: Triumph and Tears at the Judgement Seat of Christ* (Chicago, IL: Moody Publishers, 2015).

Lesson 22: Signs of the Times — David R. Reagan, *Living on Borrowed Time: The Imminent Return of Jesus* (McKinney, TX: Lamb & Lion Ministries, 2013).

Lesson 23: Death — David R. Reagan, *Eternity: Heaven or Hell?* (McKinney, TX: Lamb & Lion Ministries, 2010).

Lesson 24: A Summary Overview: David R. Reagan, *God's Plan for the Ages* (McKinney, TX: Lamb & Lion Ministries, 2005). Also: Mark Hitchcock, *The End* (Carol Stream, IL: Tyndale House Publishers, 2012).

The Authors

Darryl Nunnelley and Dave Reagan

Darryl Nunnelley is a native of the state of Kentucky. He spent three years in the 101st Airborne, with one year of service in Vietnam. He then attended the University of Kentucky where he earned a degree in Agronomy. After working seven years with the USDA Soil Conservation Service, he opened a general contracting firm. Twenty years later, in 1996, he became a hotelier and continues in that career today. Darryl became a Christian at age ten and began teaching the Bible in earnest at age 22. Since that time he has taught and preached in 13 countries, focusing most of his effort in Africa, where he has taught at Christian schools, Bible colleges and pastor conferences. He has provided scholarships to over 120 students at a seminary in Kenya. Darryl has two children and five grandchildren.

Dave Reagan is a native of Texas. He attended the University of Texas at Austin where he majored in Government and History. After being awarded a Woodrow Wilson Scholarship, he attended a Harvard graduate school where he earned a doctorate in International Law and Politics. After teaching for 20 years at several colleges and universities, he founded Lamb & Lion Ministries in 1980 for the purpose of teaching the fundamentals of Bible prophecy and proclaiming the soon return of Jesus. Since that time he has held Bible prophecy conferences all across the United States and around the world. He is the author of 15 books, and he serves as the host of the ministry's television program called "Christ in Prophecy," which is broadcast both nationally and internationally. He and his wife, Ann, have been married for almost 60 years. They have two daughters, four grandchildren and two great grandchildren.